Retreat and Retribution in Afghanistan, 1842

Retreat and Retribution in Afghanistan, 1842

Two Journals of the

First Afghan War

Margaret Kekewich

Pen & Sword
MILITARY

First published in Great Britain in 2011 by
Pen & Sword Military
An imprint of
Pen & Sword Books Ltd
47 Church Street
Barnsley
South Yorkshire
S70 2AS

Copyright © Margaret Kekewich 2011

ISBN 978 1 84884 397 4

A CIP catalogue record for this book is
available from the British Library

Typeset by Acredula

Printed and bound in England
by CPI

Pen & Sword Books Ltd incorporates the imprints of Pen & Sword Aviation,
Pen & Sword Family History, Pen & Sword Maritime, Pen & Sword Military,
Wharncliffe Local History, Pen & Sword Select, Pen & Sword Military Classics,
Leo Cooper, Remember When, Seaforth Publishing and Frontline Publishing

For a complete list of Pen & Sword titles please contact
PEN & SWORD BOOKS LIMITED
47 Church Street, Barnsley, South Yorkshire, S70 2AS, England
E-mail: enquiries@pen-and-sword.co.uk
Website: www.pen-and-sword.co.uk

Contents

To the British Armed Forces

List of Illustrations

Preface

The idea for this book originated in the discovery of a little-known *Diary* of the final stages of the First Afghan War by the Reverend Isaac Allen, it is complementary to the well-known *Journal* by Lady Florentia Sale, so the two have been combined into a narrative. I am most grateful to the staff of the British Library and the National Army Museum for their help and advice. The Somerset Military Museum is currently closed for refurbishment but the staff have kindly provided some excellent illustrations portraying the Sales. A number of friends have given me welcome support, especially Ken and Jean Lewis, Liz Saxon, Phillip Judge, who drew the maps, Malcolm Summers, Lesley Daimond and Gladys Bland. Rupert Harding, Commissioning Editor at Pen and Sword, has been prompt and positive in all our dealings and I am most grateful. It has been a pleasure to work with Alison Miles, the copy editor. It is hard to express the size of the debt that I owe to my husband, Peter Fawcett, who has sustained me in so many ways throughout this project.

Chelsea
June 2010

Major place names in the text have been modernised, those in quotations retain their original spelling, more obscure places are usually spelt as they occur in the journals.

Timeline

1838

Start of First Afghan War.

10 December: 'army of the Indus' leaves Ferozepore on Indian N.W. frontier for Afghanistan.

1839

23 July: fortress of Ghazni captured by British army.

7 August: Kabul taken and Shah Shujah installed as king. Shah Dost Mohammed flees.

September–October: most of British army returns to India.

1841

June/August: fall of Whig government led by Lord Melbourne, new Tory government led by Sir Robert Peel.

2 November: murder of Sir Alexander Burnes in Kabul. Revolt against Shah Shujah and British begins.

12 November: General Sir Robert Sale takes Jalalabad.

23 December: murder of Sir William Macnaghten, the political envoy, by Akbar Khan.

1842

6 January: General Elphinstone, the British army (4,500) and camp followers (12,000) leave Kabul.

9 January: married officers, their wives and other European women and children taken into protective custody by Akbar Khan, sent to Laghman valley.

11–13 January: last of British army destroyed at Jugdulluk and Gandamack.

13 January: only Dr Brydon reaches Jalalabad.

March: surrender of Ghazni to Akbar Khan.

7 April: General Sale wins a battle outside Jalalabad. Forces of Akbar Khan fall back on Kabul.

15 April: General Pollock's army arrives at Jalalabad.

10 May: General England enters Kandahar to reinforce General Nott's garrison.

24 May: Lady Sale and most of prisoners arrive at Kabul.

7 August: General Nott's army leaves Kandahar to return to India via Kabul.

20 August: General Pollock's army leaves Jalalabad to return to India via Kabul.

25 August: Lady Sale and most of the prisoners sent to Bamian.

6 September: General Nott recaptures Ghazni.

15 September: General Pollock retakes Kabul without resistance, some prisoners recovered.

17 September: General Nott's army arrives in Kabul.

18 September: most prisoners released.

27 September: last prisoner released.

12 October: after looting and destruction 'army of retribution' leaves Kabul.

23 December: army received with great ceremony and acclamation at Ferozepore by the Governor General of India, Lord Ellenborough.

1843

August: Sind annexed to British India.

1849

Punjab annexed to British India after Second Sikh War.

1878–80

Second Afghan War: after suffering several reverses British leave Afghanistan with a strong and friendly ruler, Abdur Rahman, in control.

1919

Third Afghan War: Afghan offensive quickly quelled by British but they recognise that it is an independent country.

Maps

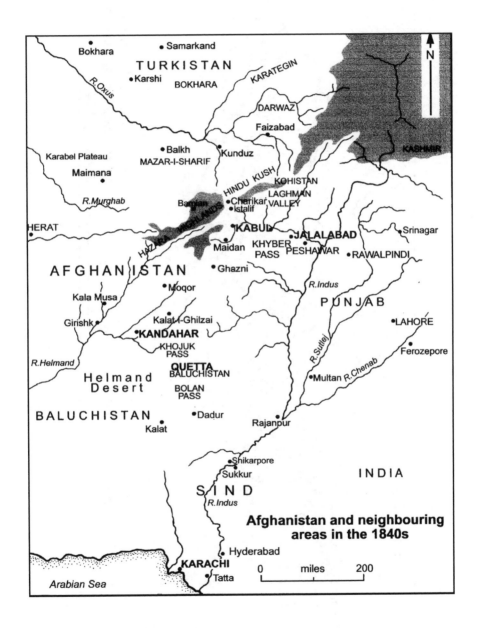

Afghanistan and neighbouring areas in the 1840s

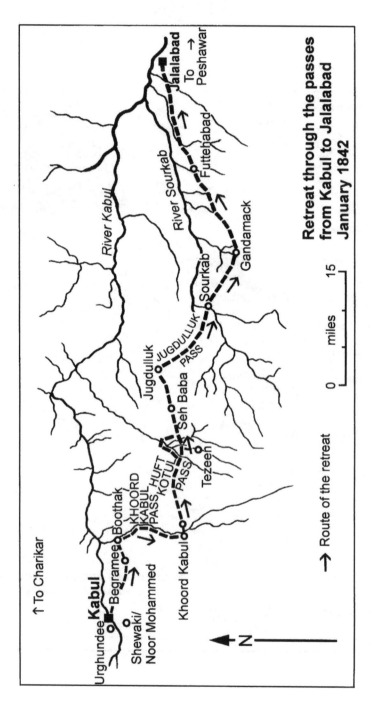

Retreat through the passes
from Kabul to Jalalabad
January 1842

→ Route of the retreat

Introduction

If we are not to repeat the bloody mistakes of the past in Afghanistan we must learn about its history

General Sir Michael Rose, 2002

The blow to British pride and confidence delivered by the defeat of their army during its retreat from Kabul in Afghanistan in January 1842 may be compared in its impact to the disaster in New York on 11 September 2001. The Prime Minister, Sir Robert Peel, and the Governor General of India, Lord Ellenborough, were torn between the desire for retribution and fears of a further disaster. The generals on the ground successfully pressed for a campaign to penetrate as far as Kabul to punish the Afghans and rescue the captive British officers and their families: a similar impulse, perhaps, to the recent desire of the US and its allies to punish the Taliban for harbouring their enemies.

Much of the history of the later stages of the first Afghan War is encapsulated in the journals of two of the participants. Lady Florentia Sale was the wife of General Sir Robert Sale, 'Fighting Bob', one of the few commanders who remained undefeated in 1842. She described in her *Journal* the deteriorating situation in Kabul, her journey accompanying the retreat of the British army through the passes from Kabul in early January 1842, then as a captive in the mountains, followed by the return to Kabul and then to Bamian where she and her companions were released eight months later. The Reverend Isaac Allen recorded his journey in his *Diary*

1

as he went first as chaplain to General William Nott's force in Kandahar and then with his army that fought its way to Kabul from August to September 1842 where they joined General Pollock's army that had previously relieved General Sale at Jalalabad. Only staying in Kabul long enough to rescue the prisoners and destroy part of the city as an exemplary punishment, the whole force withdrew from Afghanistan to India, via the Khyber pass, before the worst of the winter set in. Allen recorded their welcome back to India by Lord Ellenborough who was delighted that some honour had been rescued from the ruins of defeat.

* * *

From the late seventeenth century the partnership between the British Crown and the East India Company had progressively delivered the major part of India to their rule either directly or through alliances with Indian princes. This was supported by a large British army composed of thousands of European foot, cavalry and artillery soldiers and even larger numbers of Indian troops. The North West Frontier, however, presented several threats to security: the Sikh control of the Punjab interposed a volatile and warlike people between British India and Afghanistan. That country was controlled by a number of mutually hostile princes or warlords, most notably Shah Dost Mohammed of the Barukzai dynasty, the King of Kabul, a forebear of the last King of Afghanistan, Mohammed Zahir Shah who ruled until 1973 and died in 2007.

By the 1830s the complex relationships between the various rulers in Afghanistan, the Shah of Persia (Iran) and the British and Russian empires threatened to destabilise the region. The situation marked the beginning of 'The Great Game', as one of the political agents (British army officers who liaised with local rulers) called it. 'The Game' involved Russia and Britain attempting by diplomacy, trade, bribery and military force to gain power and influence in that area. The Russians were motivated by the wish to extend their empire southwards, the British by the need to protect their interests in India. Several factors sparked off their invasion of Afghanistan in late 1838: the fear of Russian influence; the Shah of Persia's attempt to seize the city of Herat from the Afghans and the animosity that existed between Britain's Sikh ally, Ranjit Singh (ruler of the Punjab), and Dost Mohammed. The Sikh ruler had recently seized Peshawar from the Afghans, intensifying their hatred of him.

The British held the mistaken belief that the Afghans would welcome the restoration of a former ruler in Kabul, Shah Shujah-al-Mukh of the Sadozai dynasty. He had been deposed thirty years earlier and lived in comfortable exile in India under British protection. The idea was not supported by Alexander Burnes, a political agent who had travelled extensively in the region, spoke fluent Persian and had formed a high opinion of the abilities of Dost Mohammed. An ambitious officer, Burnes suppressed his true opinion in the face of the enthusiasm for regime change shown by Lord Auckland, the Governor General of India, and his adviser Sir William Macnaghten. This misjudgement was to destroy the reputation of Auckland and the lives of Burnes, Macnaghten and many others.

'The army of the Indus' set out from northern India in December 1838 commanded by Sir John Keane. It included contingents led by Shah Shujah and the Sikhs (who soon withdrew) as well as sepoy and sowar (Indian infantry and cavalry soldiers) and British regiments, approximately 9,500 men plus about 38,000 servants and camp followers. These included handlers for the 30,000 camels plus grass-cutters for the large number of beasts that also included ponies, asses, bullocks and horses: one officer kept two camels just to carry his cigars. The logistics of leading and feeding such a large and diverse force in harsh weather over very difficult terrain and through high passes were considerable. The army encountered stiff opposition, especially at the great fortress of Ghazni, but once that had been taken the road to Kabul was open.

Shah Shujah was established as ruler in August 1839 and occupied the palace/fortress of the Bala Hissar in Kabul: Dost Mohammed fled and later surrendered to go into exile in India (Illustration 1). The British appeared to have achieved all their objectives although they found no trace of the Russian influence that they had feared (readers will be reminded of the non-existent 'weapons of mass destruction' in Iraq in 2003). Most of the army under Sir John Keane returned to India leaving garrisons in Kandahar, Kalat-i-Ghilzai, Bamian, Charikar and Ghazni. In Kabul Sir William Macnaghten, a chilly intellectual with an inflated idea of his own sagacity, was the envoy with political authority. General William Elphinstone was appointed by Lord Auckland (in 1841) a sickly and indecisive commander of two brigades: 5,000 sepoys and British soldiers, whilst Alexander Burnes was knighted and became the resident in Kabul. All was well for the first two years but the Afghans resented the British presence and never developed any respect for Shah Shujah. In the words of the Reverend Gleig, principal chaplain to the forces who published his history in 1846: 'There was no increase of good feeling on the part of the inhabitants towards the invaders. The province submitted, or appeared to submit, to Shah Shujah, but of enthusiasm in his cause no class of society exhibited a sign; while the bearing of all their intercourse with the English was as hostile as ever.' (Gleig, 39).

The directors of the East India Company and the Governor General were appalled at the continuing cost of maintaining Shah Shujah and the army that protected him in Afghanistan. Macnaghten was ordered to cut down his expenses and he halved the subsidies paid to the tribes that dominated the passes that led to and from India and controlled the hinterland of Kabul. Many Afghan chiefs had already found that the authority that they had always exercised over their lands had been usurped by the presence of the British army acting in the name of Shah Shujah. The result was unrest and a few murders culminating with the assassination of Sir Alexander Burnes in his house in Kabul on 2 November 1841. This was the signal for an uprising of the Afghans, and the *cantonments* (semi-permanent military stations) were constantly attacked causing many British casualties and their treasury and food stores were looted. In this vulnerable situation, despite the early onset of a harsh winter, Macnaghten, Elphinstone and his senior officers started negotiations to withdraw to India through the passes.

Akbar Khan, the favourite son of Dost Mohammed, appeared on the scene and became the leader of the hostile chieftains. He drove a hard bargain demanding hostages, money and most of the army's heavy guns, in return he guaranteed that it could leave Afghanistan without being attacked. Sir William Macnaghten met him on 23 December to clinch the deal but was murdered by Akbar and some of his fanatical followers. Despite this blatant act of bad faith the gullible General Elphinstone concluded an agreement with Akbar and the chiefs for the total withdrawal of the British army from the country. Shah Shujah had the choice of accompanying them or remaining in the comparative safety of the Bala Hissar and he took the second option.

On 6 January 1842 the British army and its many camp followers straggled out of the cantonments already weakened by months of scanty rations and with inadequate transport for their few guns, supplies and with clothing, in many cases, unsuited to the harsh winter weather. The story of the disaster that ensued is well known and Lady Sale and some of her fellow survivors told it graphically. Most histories of the period gloss over the subsequent imprisonment of the European women and children and some officers, troops and their servants in a few sentences. Lady Sale, however, and fellow captives, Captains Mackenzie and Lawrence and Lieutenant Eyre, provide details that illuminate the developing political situation and the Afghan mentality, since they had a great deal of personal contact with Akbar, his allies and other less-committed chieftains. The prisoners, for example, were constantly fed incorrect information about the situation in India, Kandahar, Ghazni and, especially, Jalalabad by their captors in the hope that they would prevail upon Sale to leave the town. Officers such as Captain Mackenzie were allowed to come and go as negotiators between Jalalabad and the prisoners in the spring and summer of 1842 and this had an impact on the situation, especially after the arrival there of General Pollock in mid-April.

Correspondence between Lady Sale and her husband runs as a *leitmotif* through her *Journal* for nearly a year. In some ways it was as influential on the developing situation as her letters and *Journal* that were read by the Governor General and the directors of the East India Company and published in India and England. In Jalalabad the political agent, Captain Macgregor, and clever officers like Captains Havelock and Broadfoot probably prevailed upon the general to seed in all sorts of propaganda. Conversely political agents imprisoned with Lady Sale, Major Pottinger and Captains Mackenzie and Lawrence, probably gave her their opinions about what it was wise to report to Sale. The domestic details of the imprisonment are also compelling, giving a unique insight into the living conditions and attitudes of a small group of European men, women and children who were in the power of the Afghan chieftains.

The Reverend Allen's *Diary* was little known and not used for any major accounts of the war in the nineteenth century or subsequently. He was by no means a 'yes-man', criticising the politicians whose folly had led to so many British, Indian and Afghan deaths. He praised the courage, generosity and good humour of his fellow soldiers (he counted as an officer) but could castigate snobbery and brutality when he saw it. He sincerely admired the courage and professionalism of General Nott without being blind to at least one of his shortcomings: his failure always to give due credit to the achievements of his subordinates. Allen was a gifted amateur artist and left some fine sketches and many written descriptions of what he saw, but if a portrait of him ever existed it is not known to survive. Unlike Lady Sale, he had little contact with Afghans but his account of camp life and the attitudes of his fellow officers and their men to the campaign is invaluable.

There were two major aspects of the war, however, that Allen and Lady Sale, who was deliberately misled by her captors, were not in a position to report: the siege of Jalalabad where 'Fighting Bob' Sale defeated the vastly superior forces of Akbar Khan in early April and Pollock's arrival there later in the month and subsequent advance on Kabul. Elphinstone was dead and Pollock became the senior commander on the campaign. A lively correspondence was maintained between the senior generals, Pollock and Nott, who was defending Kandahar, and Lord Ellenborough, Governor General since February 1842, in India. He was torn between his desire to deliver exemplary punishment to the Afghans and fear that the attempt to do so would end in another humiliating disaster.

Nott and Pollock, however, were made of sterner stuff than Elphinstone and they had also learnt from his mistakes. The camp followers to their armies had been scaled down, improving discipline and reducing the provisions required and the camels (invariably in short supply) to carry them. They were better supplied with food than either the original force of 1838 or the refugees from Kabul in January 1842, and although they were marching in harsh conditions they avoided the worst of the winter. They had also learnt that it was essential to 'crown the heights' if their forces were to make progress through the passes and hilly regions of the country. The various tribes that fired down on the British found that they were rapidly displaced by small detachments of their enemy that had been ordered up to beat them at their own game. Ellenborough was given sufficient confidence by the relief of Jalalabad and a few small victories to allow his generals to choose whether they would withdraw from Afghanistan by way of Quetta and Peshawar or via Kabul. A glance at the map will show that this was offering them the options of taking routes back to India avoiding the concentration of their enemies in and around Kabul, or of prolonging the campaign by attacking it. Nott had written on 2 June 'How I should like to go to Cabul!' In early August 1842 he had his wish leading his army out of Kandahar towards that city.

Both Pollock's army from Jalalabad and Nott's army from Kandahar encountered stiff opposition during their march to Kabul which they overcame with acceptably low levels of casualties. Once they arrived they faced the problem of what to do with the surviving sons of Shah Shujah since the British government had no intention of remaining in Afghanistan to support them. All but the youngest decided to leave with the army for impecunious exile in India. Pollock sent columns to wreak vengeance on the Kohistan, an area prominent in the revolt of the previous year. Villages were ruthlessly sacked, especially if they were found to contain loot taken from Elphinstone's retreating army in January (Tanner, 200). If possible, Afghan hatred of the British infidels was intensified. As soon as the European prisoners had all been recovered, Pollock planned his departure, via Jalalabad, for India but he needed to demonstrate British power and disgust at the atrocities and broken faith that had led to their defeat early in the year. Allen was horrified at the destruction of the Great Bazaar and the looting that followed but admitted that, since it was where the mangled remains of Sir William Macnaghten had been displayed, the former was probably inevitable.

Allen left Kabul in early October with the combined forces of Nott and Pollock, including General and Lady Sale, and suffered further distress at the sight of the bodies of those who had died during the previous winter's retreat. More deaths occurred as the tribesmen of the Khyber harried and robbed the stragglers from 'the army of retribution'. It is clear, however, both from Allen's account and those of his fellow officers who kept journals that the return to India was not a disorderly retreat, as was claimed by some writers and politicians at the time, but a calculated and disciplined withdrawal with acceptable levels of casualties. Like many observers Allen had mixed feelings about Ellenborough's magnificent reception of the army at Ferozepore on 23 December 1842, although he was impressed by the splendour of the occasion.

* * *

We live in a time when most aspects of Britain's former Empire and those who served it are invariably condemned. This is the prevailing assumption, for example, in Philip Hensher's engrossing novel *The Mulberry Empire*, which deals with the years leading up to the catastrophe in Kabul. The only people who are portrayed sympathetically are Alexander Burnes and some of the Afghans (the Sales are harshly treated). The contemporary accounts of the tragedy, however, give a surprisingly nuanced picture of events: Lady Sale showed concern for the unfortunate servants and the sepoys who suffered and died in huge numbers as well as for her family and the British officers. She was aware of the impact of her letters and *Journal* as they were published in India and in England and was indignant when she was misrepresented as being too lenient in her opinion of Akbar Khan. The wife of one of the few commanders who emerged with credit from the war, she could afford to express herself robustly. Both before and during the retreat from Kabul she made her disgust at the suffering caused by foolish policies and lack of leadership manifest.

The Reverend Allen was a junior member of the Anglican Church and the army but he made his dislike of the retribution business clear. Yet he recognised the need to go as far as Kabul to rescue the prisoners and also felt that the excellent qualities of his fellow officers and the soldiers were often ignored. He was irate that the return to India was misrepresented in the press as a flight rather than an orderly retreat: 'I have not hesitated to express censure where I thought it deserved, and have felt it equally a duty to repel unmerited reproach.' (*Diary*, 381). His delight in the beauty of the country and concern for the ordinary people caught up in a ruinous war rings true. He never achieved much promotion after his return to India and this could have been connected with his trenchantly expressed views.

Both accounts were published just after the war finished, in 1843: they offer modern politicians and soldiers a still relevant insight into the dangerous and intriguing enigma that is Afghanistan. This book has been written very much with the British and Allied soldiers and administrators, who are likely to be there for some time, in mind. It attempts to give a brief background to the beginnings of British involvement, the mistakes we made and the legacy that has been left to the Afghan people, through the eyes of two intelligent and outspoken people who were in great danger but who survived.

PART I

LADY FLORENTIA SALE'S *JOURNAL*, SEPTEMBER 1841 TO SEPTEMBER 1842

CHAPTER 1

Kabul, 'My Sweetpeas and Geraniums were Much Admired'

The British army and its dependants in Kabul were living on borrowed time by the autumn of 1841. Their quarters were vulnerable to attack and they had only insecure means of supplying themselves with food and other necessities. They were badly led by men who thought they could trust the tribal leaders and should negotiate with them while, in fact, their best hope of survival was to show their strength and resolution in the face of the growing disaffection of the Afghan population.

By the summer of 1841 a few European wives had joined their husbands, bringing their children with them. Sir William Macnaghten, the envoy and senior representative of the British government, had persuaded himself that the situation was stable and that the Afghans had accepted the rule of the restored king, Shah Shujah. Kabul was a pleasant place praised in 1819 by the writer and Governor of Bombay, Mountstuart Elphinstone, for its situation amongst low hills, its climate, flowers and fruit. Surrounded by a wall, the city was divided by the Kabul river: most houses were built of wood to reduce the impact of earthquakes and roofed in mud. Four bazaars converged on its central square (the Great Bazaar) and an abundance of delectable goods such as carpets, fabrics, spices and food could be purchased there. The tomb of the Emperor Babur (founder of the Moghul Empire in India; he died in 1530) stood on a hill overlooking the city surrounded by fields of anenomes, and was just the place for picnics.

The little British community of merchants and civil servants, officers and their ladies led by Sir William and Lady Fanny Macnaghten, General Elphinstone and the Sales enjoyed all the pleasures that the city offered. There were hunting parties, cricket matches, shopping, dinners and excursions. Most of these activities would have been regarded by the majority of Afghans as bizarre or vaguely irreligious. The farmers and merchants who sold their wares for good prices welcomed the foreigners (*feringhees*) and some educated Afghans enjoyed the company of the Westerners. Others, especially the fanatical Muslims (*ghazis*), detested their presence and stirred up hatred against them. Kaye (vol. 2, 143) believed that this was increased by the British soldiers themselves, some of whom seduced Afghan wives. Given the seclusion of most women it is hard to believe that this practice was widespread but historians know that rumour is often as potent a force as fact.

Lady Florentia Sale, who was in her early fifties, had arrived with one of her five surviving children, Alexandrina, in late 1839 to join her husband, Major General Sir Robert Sale, Elphinstone's second in command in Kabul. Their daughter married Captain John Sturt, a capable young engineer officer, in August 1841. Lady Sale had a high opinion of his judgement and it was partly through his eyes that the events of the remaining months in Kabul were reported in her *Journal*. She started to write in September 1841 and it became and has remained a major source for the events of the following months; and from at least October 1841 she intended it for wider consumption. It was initially compiled to inform her husband of the situation (he was absent from Kabul from 13 October) but rapidly her indignation at the way in which affairs were being mismanaged led her to write for the British government and newspapers in India and Britain. These communications were first in the form of letters but much of the information they contained had been incorporated into her *Journal* (the only item she managed to save during the retreat in January 1842) by the time it was published in 1843. She drew on the accounts of other officers as well as her own observations and recollections, including the journals of Captain Johnson which were also read by the Reverend Allen.

Initially all went well: the Sales took the best house in the *cantonments* originally occupied by the former commander, Sir John Keane, and Lady

Sale was pleased with the feminine additions that she made to it. She grew flowers that were much admired by the Afghan gentlemen who visited them, while Sir Robert devoted himself to his favourite hobby, his kitchen garden. It contained fine peas, potatoes, cauliflowers, radishes, cabbages, artichokes and turnips, although the local lettuces were dismissed as being too hairy. He can have enjoyed few opportunities for gardening during his long and distinguished career which had started in India in the late eighteenth century. He had married Florentia Wynch in 1809 in India and had subsequently served in Mauritius, Ireland and Burma and then in various Indian garrisons: he always displayed outstanding gallantry and this made him popular with his men who nicknamed him 'Fighting Bob' (Illustration 2). Man and wife had spent little time in England, Lady Sale uses Hindi and English interchangeably in her *Journal* and probably regarded India as her true home (Illustration 3). Sale had led a brigade when the 'army of the Indus' started its invasion in late 1838. He showed conspicuous gallantry, as was his custom, and was promoted to the rank of major-general and given a KCB in July 1839 when he was aged fifty-seven.

The British army both in Kabul and its garrisons elsewhere was composed of a mixture of native (Indian) and European regiments, the former were commanded by British officers and native NCOs and were employed by the East India Company. Their infantry soldiers were called 'sepoys' and their cavalry 'sowars', the infantry regiments are described as 'Native Infantry'. European regiments were employed by the British government under the commander-in-chief in India, Sir Jasper Nicholls, they are described as 'Her Majesty's'. It was intended that a small part of the original army would remain in Afghanistan, supplemented by Shah Shujah's troops. On paper he had an impressive force of about 6,000 and some of his regiments were commanded by British officers under Brigadier Anquetil. In the autumn of 1841 the envoy and his wife were to return to India to take up his new post as Governor of Bombay accompanied by soldiers, including General Sale, whose tour of duty in Afghanistan had ended. Sir Alexander Burnes, who would probably be the next envoy, was to stay and work with the Shah. General Nott from the Kandahar garrison would replace the ailing Elphinstone (also returning to India) as commander-in-chief. Nott could have been given the post in 1840 had he not alienated his superiors: they recognised his qualities as a general but doubted his diplomatic abilities. He had, for example, flogged some unruly followers of Prince Timur, the eldest son of Shah Shujah, much to Lord Auckland's annoyance (Illustration 13).

During the summer of 1841 there had been sporadic uprisings and feuds but Macnaghten was not troubled by these. One of the causes of the unrest was that he had been instructed by the East India Company to cut the enormous costs of the occupation of Afghanistan by reducing the payments given to the Ghilzai tribes, who had been bribed to keep the high passes open between Kabul, Jalalabad and the Indian frontier. Small British forces had been sent from Kabul and Kandahar into the Kohistan and Helmand areas and suppressed the disorder so Macnaghten assumed that all was well. He also knew that intertribal conflict was endemic in the country and believed that he could exploit this by turning one faction against another. He was an excellent linguist, fluent in Arabic, Persian and Sanskrit and was supremely confident that he could play the tribal chiefs at their own game.

About 5,000 European soldiers and sepoys were stationed in the *cantonments* and in a camp nearby at Siah Sung, and from time to time small numbers were also resident in Shah Shujah's palace castle of the Bala Hissar on a hill at the edge of the city. The *cantonments* (Illustration 5) contained the residency where the Macnaghtens lived as well as the officers' quarters and the Sales' house. The troops and non-commissioned officers were housed in barracks that were mostly made of wood and in tents. The whole development had cost a great deal of money to build but it was badly sited on a plain commanded by low hills, surrounded by gardens and the small forts that were a common feature of the Afghan landscape but that exposed the British to hostile fire. The buildings in the *cantonments* were extensive and, if attacked, the resources of the army would be stretched to defend their low and inadequate walls. Whilst the population remained friendly the army was well placed to trade for food with farmers and merchants, it even kept its main supplies in a fort some distance from the *cantonments* and much of its treasure was in a house in the city.

By early October the persistent unrest in the vicinity of Kabul could not be ignored. Macnaghten and the sickly commander of the army, Major General William Elphinstone, were both desperate to leave Afghanistan. General Sale was sent with a brigade which left for Boothak between 9 and 13 of the month both to cow the surrounding tribes and to prepare the way through the passes for the departing leaders: Sir Robert expected his wife to join him 'in three days at the latest'. Because it was thought that they were going directly to India Sale's men were given the most ancient muskets from the munitions store. He entered the Khoord Kabul pass, which was bristling with hostile Afghans, to secure an advanced position before falling back on Boothak. The manoeuvre was successful but very costly in lives and Sale was badly wounded in the left leg near his ankle. He was confined to a litter but insisted on getting up from time to time, such activity did not hasten his recovery and he refused to return to Kabul with most of the wounded. Lieutenant Mein, who was later to accompany and protect Lady Sale on the retreat, had his skull fractured by a ball and was laid up in Kabul for the rest of the year. Relatively few Afghans had managed to inflict such serious damage on the British by firing down on them from the heights, a terrible foretaste of what was to come. The enemy had certainly not been cowed.

Dispiriting news arrived at this time: Mrs Smith, the wife of a conductor (NCOs charged with obtaining army supplies), had been murdered in the Bolan Pass on her way to Kandahar. Lady Sale thought that the Baluchis who did the deed had initially mistaken her for a man when she fled from them as her body was neither violated nor plundered and women were normally respected. Kandahar, the strategic fortified city on the road to the passes that led to the Indian frontier, was held for Britain by the formidable Major General William Nott who had a division of about 3,000 men there. He was the ablest and most ruthless commander in Afghanistan and as the intended replacement for Elphinstone could probably have held out in Kabul. It was a tragedy for the British that events prevented this from happening. Garrisons also held Ghazni, not far from Kabul, Kalat-i-Ghilzai near Kandahar, and a few minor posts. Meanwhile, Sale's brigade had been attacked at Tezeen with more men killed and wounded.

Many of the British felt that everything was under control, they included Macnaghten who: 'is trying to deceive himself into an assurance that the country is in a quiescent state' (*Journal*, 22). So optimistic were they that: 'it was generally understood, that all [British troops] should be withdrawn as soon as the Shah had raised five more regiments of his own' (*Journal*, 23). Lady Sale, however, put no trust in the good faith of the chiefs upon whose support such arrangements depended. The constant small hostilities against the British in and around Kabul justified her pessimism.

Lady Sale was pleased to receive a letter from 'her husband on 28 October in which he reported that his wound was less inflamed. His brigade had moved to a more comfortable position at Seh Baba where a chief was helping them to get good supplies of food and fodder. He may have been trying to cheer her up as she learnt from other officers that they were subject to periodic attacks, several officers and men had been killed or wounded and frequent attempts were made to plunder the force. The chiefs blamed brigands but Captain Macgregor, the political agent accompanying Sale, suspected that the chiefs were involved despite all their promises and the bribes that they were receiving. Attacks were also being made on British soldiers around the Kabul *cantonments*, but plans were still afoot to evacuate all the sick and wounded who would accompany the Macnaghtens and Elphinstone when they returned to India. On 30 October Sale wrote to his superiors warmly commending the perseverance and bravery of his officers and men who had endured days of hard fighting and bivouacking at night in the cold passes. He singled out Colonels Dennie and Montieth and Captains Wade, Abbott and Havelock for special mention (Low, 213–14).

Bad news arrived from Sale's brigade on the evening of 31 October, it had been attacked between Jugdulluk and Sourkab by about 400 Afghans who had unexpectedly left the pass open. The British were unable to force the heights but went on anyway: 'Fighting Bob Sale' was a valiant but not very intelligent commander, although his wife never criticised him. His rear-guard suffered ninety killed and wounded and huge losses of baggage and camels: the latter were returned at a cost of 20 rupees (for Afghan animals) or 10 rupees (for Indian beasts) a head. Lady Sale remarked that this was a bad precedent to set but necessary given the dangerous shortage of camels. The difference in price may be explained by Captain Colin Mackenzie's observation that Indian camels often died from eating a poisonous plant, rather like a foxglove, whilst Afghan camels shunned it. (Mackenzie, vol. 1, 161).

An unpleasant (and given later events totally irrelevant) row had broken out over accommodation. There were two issues: the payment of rent for officers' quarters and Brigadier Shelton's attempt to take over the Sales' house. The East India Company was anxious to rescue what it could from the financial black hole that was Afghanistan and was asking officers who were absent on duty from Kabul to keep paying for their quarters in the *cantonments*. The Sales paid theirs regularly through the regimental paymaster so, to Lady Sale's relief, they were not involved in this wrangle. On the other hand, she detested Brigadier Shelton, a difficult, self-centred man but a brave, if unreliable, soldier. He expected Lady Sale to leave shortly and wanted to occupy either her desirable residence or Elphinstone's house. She had other plans, however:

> Now, as long as Brig. Shelton's duty keeps him at Siah Sung, he has no business in cantonments. This is Sunday: both the General and I expect to march on Wednesday, so . . . we neither of us expected to be turned out; however, if we do not go, we both intend vacating our habitations, when our house will be made over to Capt. Sturt, to undergo repairs, so as to be ready for the next Commander of the forces [Nott]
>
> (*Journal*, 28).

The two objectives of Sale's brigade – to secure the route for Elphinstone and Macnaghten's return to India and to control the local tribes – were not proving easy to accomplish. Shortage of animals was already leading to talk of leaving the sick and wounded behind in Kabul. Lady Sale was desperately worried by the end of the following day, 1 November, to have heard nothing from Sale but this was to be only the beginning of the woes of the British.

CHAPTER 2

Kabul, Disaster

The fate of the British was sealed when they failed to punish those who murdered Sir Alexander Burnes and revolted against Shah Shujah in early November 1841. The Afghans saw their weakness and constantly attacked and robbed them, and the chiefs ensured that the British were deprived of the food and fodder they needed to remain a viable force. The murder of Sir William Macnaghten, also unpunished, left the badly led army in an abject condition at the mercy of its enemies.

Friendly Afghans had been warning the British for some time to be on their guard against an uprising in Kabul. Mohan Lal, a Hindu interpreter who was a source of usually reliable information, also predicted impending trouble. Macnaghten with his love of intrigue and mastery of local languages believed himself to be equal to the situation. Elphinstone, then and later, never seemed to have had any idea of what might be done other than to leave as quickly as possible. Some officers and the envoy-in-waiting (this could have been a temporary appointment as he was not universally popular), Sir Alexander Burnes, lived in Kabul. There was something to be said for this as it enabled them to keep in closer contact with the developing situation than was possible in the withdrawn circumstances of the *cantonments*: or it should have done.

On 2 November a howling mob gathered outside the house of Alexander Burnes, he tried and failed to calm them with a speech, for he was fluent in Persian, and shooting started. Lieutenant Broadfoot (who had unfortunately been breakfasting with Burnes) and the guard were killed. Burnes and his younger brother attempted to escape through a side door in disguise but they were recognised and hacked to pieces. Hearing that Burnes and the British treasury in the city were being attacked, Elphinstone sent Captain Sturt to Shah Shujah at the Bala Hissar to concert measures for its defence but just before he entered the fortress he was attacked and stabbed deeply in the face, shoulder and side.

Lady Sale arranged for Sturt's litter to be brought to her house where her daughter was staying and they were appalled by his wounds and the quantity of blood that he had lost. He was unable to speak or swallow and after a doctor had dressed his wounds Alexandrina spent hours removing blood from his mouth with warm, wet cloths. By late evening he could speak a little and swallow spoonfuls of water. During the day various reports reached the *cantonments* concerning Burnes, although Lady Sale thought that the notorious womaniser's only hope of safety rested: 'on the possibility of his having obtained refuge in some *harem*' (*Journal*, 35). They did hear, however, that several officers who had houses in the town were safe in the *cantonments* but that the army treasury in the city had been sacked with a loss of a *lakh* (equivalent to £10,000) and 70,000 rupees. Elphinstone had done nothing to rescue Burnes despite an urgent message from him in the morning. Shah Shujah sent Campbell's regiment into the city but it was overwhelmed and lost several of its guns. He also threatened to burn Kabul if the rebellion was not over by the following morning, not easy as Lady Sale drily remarked as: 'the houses are all flat-roofed and mud- roofed' (*Journal*, 37).

The outpost at Siah Sung was withdrawn and the Macnaghtens left their residency for the comparative safety of the military part of the *cantonments*. By nightfall on 2 November it was accepted by most of the British that Burnes must be dead; but good news did arrive from Sale at Gandamack, he was receiving support from the local chiefs and was well supplied. The following day Captain Trevor, his wife and seven children managed to escape from the isolated fort where they lived but only with the clothes they stood up in. The 37th Bengal Regiment Native Infantry from Sale's brigade was sent back from Khoord Kabul, in response to an order from Elphinstone, to strengthen the forces in the face of the rebellion. They were fiercely attacked but arrived in good order, although this meant that, two months later, most of them would die on the retreat from Kabul whereas they would otherwise have remained under the command of General Sale in Jalalabad. Some soldiers and supplies were sent to the Bala

Hissar to sustain the king. The prospects for a peaceful departure for the envoy and Elphinstone, accompanied by Lady Sale, were looking ever blacker.

During the following two months Lady Sale described the deteriorating situation of the British in Kabul with grim resignation and some humour. In the first few days after the rebellion they lost several forts that were strategically placed in the vicinity of the *cantonments* and these made excellent bases from which the Afghans could fire on the beleaguered British troops. It also sent a clear message to neutral or friendly factions and tribes, such as the Kuzzilbashis (Persian speakers and Shia unlike the Sunni Afghan majority) that British power was waning and not worth supporting. Dispiriting numbers of officers and men were killed and wounded, although Sturt had recovered sufficiently to give good advice from his sickbed which was duly ignored.

The most dangerous loss occurred on 5 November when the unfortunate lieutenant who was defending the commissariat fort had to abandon it in face of many desertions and Elphinstone's failure to reinforce him. Not only did this mean the loss of staple supplies but also of rum (good for morale) and medical stores of sago, arrowroot and wine. Rations were cut in the *cantonments* with further loss of morale and fitness to fight and the soldiers had to spend long hours outside protecting the *cantonments* and suffering greatly from the cold. A number contracted pneumonia: although there was a good store of wood, despite Sturt's entreaties, the men were not allowed to light fires to warm themselves. Lady Sale castigated the officers who did not share these hardships but singled out Captain Bygrave, the paymaster-general, for praise as he never slept away from his post.

Lady Sale made a good analysis at this time of the reasons for the superiority of the Afghans over the British in the various engagements that were fought at Kabul:

> Each horseman takes a foot soldier up behind him, and drops him when he is arrived at the spot he is required to fire from. Their horsemen . . . are all well mounted, and their baggage ponies can manage the hills much better than our cavalry horses . . . As regards pistols, we are on a par, . . . but their *juzails* (long rifles) carry much

further than our muskets, and, whilst they are out of range of our fire, theirs tells murderously on us . . . I often hear Affghans designated as cowards: they are a fine manly-looking set, and I can only suppose it arises from the British idea that assassination is a cowardly act. The Affghans never scruple to use their long knives for that purpose, ergo they are cowards; but they show no cowardice in standing as they do against guns without using any themselves, and in escalading and taking forts which we cannot retake.

(*Journal*, 64, 77)

She could have added that the Afghans had the advantages of good supplies of food and ammunition and strong if not co-ordinated leadership. Captain Abbott and Lieutenant Greenwood (see Part II, Chapter 4) made the same point about the superiority of the Afghan *jezails*. The army had enjoyed nearly two years of relative calm since it invaded and could surely have addressed this basic problem of equipment during that time.

On 6 November some of the tribal leaders and *mullahs* (priests) proclaimed the Nawab Zeman Khan as their new king; he was an elderly relation of Dost Mohammed who proved to be compassionate in his later dealings with the British. He was by no means recognised by all the leaders as it served the purposes of some to remain loyal to Shah Shujah for the time being. He had sunk into deep despondency and warned the 860 ladies of his harem that, if the *cantonments* fell to his enemies, he would poison them all! Some of the British and later historians believed that he had encouraged the rebellion but, apart from letters written to pacify the menacing chiefs, there is little to support the suspicion.

There was a fierce fight on 10 November over the possession of the Rikabashees' fort, despite heavy casualties on both sides Lady Sale conceded that the commander, Brigadier Shelton, conducted himself bravely. The fort was eventually captured by the British together with four other smaller ones. This proof that they could still be formidable, despite their inaction at the beginning of the rebellion, had a sobering effect on the enemy and supplies began to come in. Lady Sale and her companions believed that either her husband or General Nott would shortly arrive to relieve them. Perhaps in recognition of Shelton's gallantry she finally relinquished her house to him on 13 November as he was 'grumbling about the cold in a tent'. She settled in the Sturts' house with her daughter, son-in-law and the severely wounded Lieutenant Mien, they were attended by about forty servants. A letter arrived from Sale at Gandamack dated 9 November making it clear, she said, that none of the messages Elphinstone had sent recalling him to Kabul had got through (*Journal*, 106). The messengers (*cossids*) who were regularly sent out by the British commanders were frequently stopped and often mutilated or killed: even when dispatches were written in French or Latin the Afghans had men educated enough to read them.

Macnaghten and Elphinstone had deluded themselves that the Kohistan had been pacified by their military action in the early autumn. All doubts on that score were dispelled on 15 November by the arrival of the political agent from Charikar, Major Eldred Pottinger, Lieutenant Haughton, both wounded, plus one gurkha and an interpreter. They were all that remained of a force of several hundred native troops (some of whom had deserted), European officers and camp followers that had attempted to retreat to Kabul after the whole country had risen against them. Pottinger was already a hero for his role in holding Herat against the Persians in 1838, and from his account of the retreat from Charikar it is astonishing that anyone survived. Haughton's right arm had been amputated before he left and the muscles in his neck had been severed so he could not keep his head upright. The arm later had to be re-amputated but that probably saved his life as he was left with the sick and wounded in Kabul in January 1842. He later achieved a distinguished career, first in the army and then in the Indian civil service: when he retired he was awarded the honorary rank of lieutenant-general.

A resourceful messenger arrived on 18 November bringing a letter confirming earlier reports that Sale, far from obeying orders from Elphinstone to return to Kabul, had proceeded with his sick and wounded to Jalalabad that he had occupied. The messenger had swallowed a smaller letter and torn the larger in three parts that he had concealed when the enemy searched him. Later in the day another letter arrived from Sale who had fought a successful action against 5,000 opponents. Lady Sale said that the only word he had received from Kabul was her letter covering events from 2 to 8 November. Brigadier Shelton annoyed her again by sarcastically remarking that her husband had gone to Jalalabad on the principle, 'Being out of a scrape, keep so'. There was considerable controversy at the time and subsequently about whether or not Sale should have returned to Kabul. Captain Abbott, who accompanied Sale to Jalalabad, categorically stated (Low, 220–2) that he received the order but chose to disobey it on the grounds that he would have to abandon 300 sick and wounded to their fate and had insufficient men and ammunition to make it back through the passes. Abbott supported his commander in this decision; he also commented on the poor state of the town's defences and the fact that they found none of the supplies that they had expected to be there. Sale's men, led by Captain Broadfoot, set about improving the fortifications and eventually Captain Macgregor, their resourceful political agent, managed to bring in some supplies. Lady Sale had written on 6 November that Elphinstone had ordered her husband to return to Kabul but then changed his mind since Sale could not guarantee the safety of the sick and wounded (*Journal*, 65–6).

Lady Sale was disgusted at the way in which Shelton and other officers engaged in defeatist talk (croaking) in front of their soldiers: 'It is more than shocking, it is shameful, to hear the way that officers go on croaking before the men: it is sufficient to dispirit them, and prevent their fighting for us' (*Journal*, 116). She followed this up with accounts of how several sepoys, including NCOs, had deserted. These desertions were to be a major problem for the British whilst they remained in Kabul and on the retreat.

From time to time officers led sorties from the *cantonments* but rarely achieved anything other than more dead and wounded. Lieutenant Eyre believed that the last chance for the British was the attempt to take the village of Beymaroo on 23 November. A main source of their scanty supplies and in an important strategic position, this was a good plan but, unfortunately, Brigadier Shelton fought the engagement as if he was at Waterloo. After losing the impact of a surprise night attack by starting too late and failing to take the village when it was lightly defended, his two hollow squares of infantrymen were drawn up in an exposed position and they were mown down by the ever greater numbers of *jezailchis* who poured out of Kabul. The one British gun became overheated and had to stop firing and a second sent up to relieve it was captured. The cavalry, hemmed in by the two infantry squares, could do little but be picked off by marksmen: Shelton had refused to throw up a breastwork (*sungah*). Badly led, the men became dispirited after hours of exposure and eventually retreated in confusion after heavy losses. No one doubted Shelton's personal courage (not diminished by the fact that he had only one arm) but his tactics were deplorable and he did not inspire his men (Eyre, *Military Operations at Cabul*, 115–31).

Lieutenant Vincent Eyre, an artillery officer, was an amateur artist who was also interested in botany, both these skills enhance the interest of his account. He had been wounded in November and was accompanied by his wife and child, circumstances that probably saved his life. His *Journal* was published in 1843 and there is considerable overlap in the material with Lady Sale's but, as an officer, he sometimes had different priorities and extracts from it complement her account. In 1842 he made a series of sketches of the European captives, including Lady Sale, which are a valuable source for their appearance and way of life in prison (Illustration 7).

Macnaghten's negotiations might have encouraged the enemy to hold their hand a little and there were still rumours of a relieving force marching either from Kandahar or from India: The 'Ghilzye chiefs say they have sworn on the Koran to fight against us; and so they must fight, but that they will not fight hard. That is what they have told Sir William through their emissaries. He is trying to treat with all parties' (*Journal*, 119).

In late November Akbar Khan, Dost Mohammed's favourite son, arrived in Kabul; he was twenty-five years old and led 6,000 men. Although Shah Zeman Khan had been proclaimed king, it was to be Akbar who by a combination of superior force and duplicity was to bring about the destruction of Elphinstone's army. He had a complex personality, sometimes chivalrous and generous, sometimes violent and avaricious but always mendacious. He admired bravery, even on the part of his enemies, and was invariably considerate towards the European ladies (Illustration 6).

The British were offered terms that they could not possibly accept: Shah Shujah was to be surrendered together with all their guns and ammunition and General Sale should retreat to Peshawar. The next day it started to snow. This could have been the reason, together with a wish to improve morale, that led the Macnaghtens to leave their tent in the *cantonments* and return to the residency.

Elphinstone had written to Nott at Kandahar in mid-November ordering him to send a brigade to relieve the hard-pressed army in Kabul. Nott complied, sending Colonel Maclaren, but with a bad grace and huge reservations that he expressed in a letter to his daughters on 17 November: 'I am obliged strictly to obey the orders of such stupid people, when I know these orders go to ruin the affairs of the British Government, and to cut the throats of my handful of soldiers and my own . . . How strange that Macnaghten has never been right, even by chance!' (Stocqueler, vol. 1, 362).

Maclaren's force was inadequate for its formidable task and did not even get as far as Ghazni: he had no useful supplies or treasure to take to Kabul and his camels and bullocks died in droves in the cold. Allen was to see the piles of their whitened bones the following August at Tazi (See Part II, Chapter 4) where Maclaren abandoned his advance and returned to Kandahar on 2 December 1841. His decision was applauded by one of Nott's Bengal officers who wrote an anonymous account of his part in the war (*Recollections*, 55). On the other hand, Lieutenant John Samuel Knox of the 42nd Bengal Regiment Native Infantry, who actually accompanied Maclaren's force, criticised the decision to withdraw: 'I could see no great or insurmountable obstacle to our advance, and I look on our return as little short of disgraceful' (*Nott's Brigade in Afghanistan*, 53).

In late November and early December there was a lull in the hostilities although sporadic firing from both sides continued. The envoy was negotiating with Akbar and the chiefs and there were rumours of divisions between the various leaders. On 4 December, however, attacks on the *cantonments* started in earnest, probably in an attempt to improve the Afghans' negotiating position. The British still hoped that Nott's men were coming to rescue them and a messenger arrived from Ghazni who swore on

27

the Koran that relief was on its way from Kandahar. Lady Sale snorted that 'he was, of course, implicitly believed'. On 8 December considerable amounts of ammunition and personal baggage being sent from the *cantonments* to the Bala Hissar were lost when the escort was attacked and most of the grooms (*saces*) ran away. 'Had Sturt's wish been complied with [he had raised this with Elphinstone on 4 November], long ago we should have been safe in the Bala Hissar, with plenty of provisions, and might have set all Affghanistan at defiance until an army could arrive from the provinces' (*Journal*, 166).

On the same day Major General Elphinstone, Brigadiers Shelton and Anquetil and Colonel Chambers, the most senior officers and 'croakers' to a man, wrote to Macnaghten complaining about the inadequacy of the *cantonments* and their provisions and urged him to negotiate the best possible terms for withdrawal from Kabul. Shelton had the strongest personality amongst the senior officers so his wish to retreat on Jalalabad predominated: when other options were being discussed in their meetings he tended to lie on the floor wrapped up in a blanket pretending to be asleep.

Macnaghten accordingly negotiated with Akbar Khan and the chiefs throughout December as it grew steadily colder. Some of the latter offered to bring Akbar's head to the envoy but he replied that assassination was not the British custom. Yet his willingness to treat with two factions simultaneously was known to the Afghans and undermined his credibility with them. A letter arrived from the garrison at Ghazni; they were besieged but believed that Colonel Maclaren was on his way from Kandahar to relieve them. Even if this had happened, on balance, it is unlikely that they would have been capable of sending much help to Kabul. The deteriorating weather, shortage of funds and lack of draught animals put all parts of the occupying British army in a perilous situation. There was talk of Shah Shujah leaving the Bala Hissar to join the retreat to India but he never came for he was sufficiently shrewd to appreciate the dangers of such a move.

The negotiations made the British unsure as to who their enemies were, Afghans milled about the entrances to the *cantonments* and robbed anyone they encountered, Hindus, Europeans or fellow Afghans. Small amounts of supplies were allowed in but everyone was on the verge of starvation and their animals were dying. The Sturts and Lady Sale did manage to buy some camels for a high price and acquired some provisions for their servants. As a sign of good will the British surrendered the Rikabashees' fort and two others on 15 December making the *cantonments* even more vulnerable. As Lady Sale morosely remarked: 'Our allies, as they are now called, will be very magnanimous if they let us escape, now that they have fairly got us in their net' (*Journal*, 182). News arrived two days later that all was well at Kalat-i-Ghilzai and Kandahar, Nott's men had concentrated the minds of local rebel chiefs by blowing one they had captured out of a gun! Knox gave a horrific account of the occasion, 'a most disgusting spectacle' (*Nott's Brigade in Afghanistan*, 43–5).

Taj Mohammed Khan, a pro-British chief, visited Sturt on 20 December bringing some welcome cheese with him but his warning to the family was stark and prophetic: that the retreating army would be annihilated. He wished to take the Sturts and Lady Sale into his protection in the hills until an avenging British army appeared. They were grateful for his offer but: 'It is difficult to make these people understand our ideas on military subjects; and how a proceeding, which was only intended to save a man's life, conjointly with that of his wife and mother, can in any way affect his honour. Certain it is that we have very little hope of saving our lives' (*Journal*, 187).

At this stage Sturt, who never tired of giving advice that was not taken, suggested to Elphinstone that they should break off negotiations, retreat to Jalalabad and await the arrival of reinforcements either there or at Peshawar. Had his advice been followed immediately a far greater proportion of the army and its followers would almost certainly have been saved. Whenever she quoted Sturt's opinion, Lady Sale supported it uncritically but, in his *Journal*, his fellow officer Lieutenant Eyre expressed his reservations about his tactical advice: both, however, were in agreement about the fatuity of the senior command.

News arrived that Colonel Maclaren's attempt to relieve Ghazni had failed and the force had fallen back on Kalat-i-Ghilzai. Elphinstone's reaction was to order the surrender of Ghazni as his army would be taking the alternative route out of Afghanistan via Jalalabad, but the garrison continued to hold out in the citadel for a few more months. The British in Kabul, anticipating an imminent departure, started to give up their wagons, ammunition and Lady Macnaghten's carriage to Akbar Khan, as well as a large sum of money. This, Lady Sale believed, made him more powerful and dangerous than before since he could purchase additional followers.

A defining stage in the long drawn-out negotiations between the British, Akbar Khan and the chiefs for the army's withdrawal was reached on 23 December. Macnaghten went out in the morning to meet Akbar on neutral ground between the *cantonments* and the Siah Sung hill. The envoy was accompanied only by ten men including Captains Trevor, Mackenzie and Lawrence; the military escort that should have been provided by Elphinstone had failed to arrive in time. For a while Macnaghten sat on the ground with Akbar and some of the chiefs but he was later seized and shot with a fine pistol that he had previously presented to the *Sirdar* (General). Trevor was pulled from his horse and murdered but Mackenzie (who had always suspected a plot) and Lawrence were protected by some of the chiefs and escaped, remaining for a time in the city; Captain Skinner also stayed there in hiding.

The first Lady Sale knew of the matter was: 'About two o'clock we suddenly heard firing, and all went to the rear gate to see what the matter was; when I met Mr Waller [Lieutenant Robert Waller] who informed me that the Envoy had been taken away by the chiefs' (*Journal*, 194). Later in the day they could see: 'a great crowd round a body, which the Affghans were seen to strip: it was evidently that of a European; but, strange to say, no endeavour was made to recover it, which might easily have been done by sending out cavalry' (*Journal*, 197). Instead the envoy's body was hacked to pieces and parts were paraded about the city and displayed in Kabul's Great Bazaar (Illustration 4). The following day all hope of his survival was lost when Lady Sale received a letter from Captain Lawrence and had the painful task of informing Lady Macnaghten and Mrs Trevor that their husbands had been murdered.

The British were now in an extremely weak position: the envoy may have been deluded but at least he was capable of taking decisions. The political agents, Major Eldred Pottinger, who as the senior assumed

Macnaghten's role, Captains George Lawrence and Colin Mackenzie, were soldiers so the final authority now rested with Elphinstone, probably the most indecisive general in the Indian service. Unfortunately Akbar Khan detested Pottinger, an able negotiator, who was sidelined in the months to come. According to Lady Sale, Akbar cried for two hours to show how sorry he was for Macnaghten's death, but he could also accuse the British of duplicity for trying to play him off against the chiefs. The army's failure to rescue the envoy's body, that lay for some time a short distance from the *cantonments*, or take any other measure to punish his murder showed their fatal weakness to their enemies.

The terms of the proposed treaty became even harsher: the army's treasure must be surrendered along with all but six of their guns and married men with their families (including General Sale at Jalalabad) must be left as hostages. Lieutenant Eyre was prepared to stay with his wife and child but Captain Anderson said that he would rather shoot his wife and Sturt said that they would only take his wife and mother at the point of a bayonet. Christmas Day was a dismal affair and, although news arrived on 26 December that reinforcements were beginning to arrive at Peshawar, everyone knew that they could not possibly reach Kabul in time to save them. In the event, 'the army of retribution' did not even assemble in Afghanistan until April and early May 1842 and only set out for Kabul in August.

Elphinstone with Shelton, Anquetil, Chambers and Pottinger ratified a slightly revised treaty with Akbar Khan and the chiefs on 27 December. It was described by Lady Sale as 'most disgraceful' and involved the payment of 40,000 rupees, the surrender of all but six guns and six officers were given up as hostages, including Captains Walsh and Drummond and Lieutenant Conolly. In return Akbar Khan promised to protect the army from attack during its retreat and to arrange for it to receive supplies of food and fodder. In the subsequent narrative only the six officers surrendered in late December are referred to as 'hostages', the rest who were captured later are described as 'prisoners'.

The hostages were cheered up by Shah Zeman Khan (the alternative king) who visited them in the city with his musicians who played and sang until 11.00 pm. The sick were also sent into the city in the care of two doctors as there was insufficient transport for them to accompany the army. They were far better off there than if they had remained with the army where they would almost certainly have perished. Those who survived their illnesses and wounds enjoyed the protection of Zeman Khan until just before the arrival of Pollock's army in Kabul when they were sent to join the other prisoners.

Snow had been lying on the ground since 18 December and more had fallen during most days since then. The army's withdrawal kept being postponed by Akbar from day to day as its animals were plundered and starved and the soldiers and followers subsisted on scanty rations. On 4 January Lady Sale heard from her husband in a letter dated 19 December 1841, he only knew of events from her letter of ten days earlier. All was well in Jalalabad and he was continuing to strengthen its fortifications. He believed (wrongly) that a force was on its way from Kandahar to relieve Kabul and that the army there had plenty of rations. He had forwarded extracts from her letter to the government in India for, he wrote: 'No other person gives them any idea of our real position in Cabul' (*Journal*, 218). Captains Mackenzie and Skinner were released from the city and arrived in the *cantonments*, the latter having experienced some curious adventures, disguised as an Afghan woman.

Friendly Afghans continued to warn the Sturts and Lady Sale that they would be attacked when they left the *cantonments* despite the treaty. She and her daughter were advised to wear sheepskins (*neemchees*) and turbans and to ride amongst the troopers as the ladies in camel-panniers (*palkees*) would be easy to attack. In the meantime Sturt was busy, as the only engineer officer, in making the final arrangements for the retreat. He sloped the banks of the canal that flowed out of the river Kabul parallel to the *cantonments* to make crossing it easier for the camels. Before daylight on the day of departure he was to put up a temporary, narrow bridge over the river (the Afghans had destroyed the original one). On 5 January, when it was certain that the army would depart the following day, he made a large breach in the *cantonments'* wall so that soldiers, followers and beasts of burden could leave as quickly as possible. He did so with a heavy heart for he knew all too well the frightful conditions to which they would be exposed.

CHAPTER 3

The Retreat Through the Passes

The starving, badly equipped British army that left Kabul in deep snow on 6 January 1842 had little chance of surviving. Had it been well led by a ruthless commander several quick, long marches might have enabled the strongest to reach Jalalabad in a few days but this would have entailed abandoning the camp followers, the European women and children. Elphinstone was a weak but honourable man and, eventually, he did allow Akbar Khan to take officers accompanied by wives and other European women and children into protective custody and this saved their lives. Nearly all the European officers and troops were killed and the majority of the sepoys and camp followers died miserably or were sold into slavery.

The British retreat from Kabul, under the 'protection' of Akbar Khan, that had been so much discussed now commenced. The alternatives of remaining in the *cantonments* or taking refuge in the Bala Hissar were not considered to be viable. Difficulties in defending and provisioning the *cantonments* certainly made staying there unattractive. Holding the Bala Hissar, on the other hand, would have been preferable to a march through the passes in the depths of winter and this was the opinion of Lady Sale: 'November 4: Sturt strongly advises the troops all being thrown into the Bala Hisar, and the cantonments being abandoned until we get up reinforcements; but the cry is, how can we abandon the cantonments that have cost us so much money?' (*Journal*, 57).

The accommodation in the Bala Hissar was solid and extensive, the army would have had more ammunition than it took with it on the retreat and it retained sufficient funds to buy provisions until a relieving force arrived. Unfortunately, the ailing Elphinstone and some of the senior officers by this time disliked Afghanistan so intensely that they just wished to leave as quickly as possible. The terrible danger into which the general was leading his troops with scanty ammunition and provisions and weak animals to transport them did not seem to weigh heavily with him. The potential suffering of the thousands of sepoys and camp followers, mostly Hindus from the warm plains of India, does not appear to have been considered. Elphinstone took much of Shah Shujah's force with him, led by Brigadier Anquetil, a gross betrayal of the unfortunate monarch as he himself pointed out (Eyre, *Military Operations at Cabul*, 208). He just had to hope that he could retain the support of sufficient numbers of the tribal leaders to be able to survive in the Bala Hissar.

The long and futile negotiations between Sir William Macnaghten, Akbar Khan and the other leaders had wasted valuable time and further depleted the army's resources. A particularly early and harsh winter had set in by the time the 4,500 soldiers and approximately 12,000 servants and camp followers finally left the *cantonments* on 6 January 1842. The force consisted of 700 Europeans, these included the horse artillery and HM 44th Infantry, there were also some sappers and miners, mountain gunners, the mission escort and about 32 European women and children. There were three sepoy battalions of the East India Company's infantry, the 5th, 37th and 54th Bengal Regiments, a regiment of Bengal light cavalry, the Shah's foot and cavalry, including Anderson's, Hopkins' and Skinner's Horse and Mackenzie's Afghan riflemen (*jezailchis*). The original force had been depleted by the departure of Sale's brigade but the numbers were supplemented by the Shah's soldiers.

They started to move off at 9.30 am when the snow was a foot deep and the temperature was below freezing. The ladies were placed with the advance guard under escort but Lady Sale and her daughter preferred to ride mixed in with the cavalry. This spared them the nuisance of waiting to cross the temporary bridge over the Kabul river that was narrow and insecure. They easily forded the river nearby but there were long delays as most of the camp followers shunned the freezing water and jostled to cross the bridge. As the last troops left the *cantonments* the Afghans poured in to plunder and most of the servants carrying the baggage, provisions and ammunition threw away their loads and fled. The only thing to be saved by the Sales was Alexandrina's bedding since their nurse (*ayah*) was riding on it.

The retreat from the *cantonments* had been so disorderly that little semblance of military discipline remained: soldiers, families and camp followers were all mixed together. They had been on short rations for weeks and their animals were starving so men, women, children and beasts soon started dying in the extreme cold. Against the advice of friendly Afghans the whole force halted at 4.00 pm having only progressed 6 miles: it would have been preferable, given their lack of food and shelter, to have pressed on through the Khoord Kabul Pass. The Sturts, Lady Sale, Lieutenant Mien (who was still too weak from wounds previously acquired to fight) and the *ayah* spent an uncomfortable night with hardly any food in a small, drafty tent provided by Captain Johnson. They were more fortunate, however, than most of the army that remained starving in the open without fuel to start fires, some of the sepoys even burnt parts of their uniforms for a little temporary heat. Captain Mackenzie and twenty of his riflemen managed to avoid frostbite by clearing the snow and lying in a tight circle with their feet meeting in the middle and their fur-lined coats (*poshteens*) above and beneath them, profiting from the communal body warmth. A total of 250 of Shah Shujah's soldiers deserted together with 400 of Hopkins's men and they returned to Kabul.

The 7 January proved an even worse day since to the lack of supplies and the cold an even more deadly danger was added: Afghan attack, despite all Akbar Khan's promises. The mountain train of three-pounder guns was captured; they were later retaken but had to be spiked and left behind as the men charged with guarding them ran away. During the march two more guns were abandoned and spiked because the horses were too weak to drag them. Only two horse artillery guns and very little ammunition were left to protect the force. Its flanks were attacked and looted incessantly and many soldiers found that their hands were too cold to use their weapons. Again, Elphinstone decided to stop early at Boothak, having advanced only 5 miles, thus exposing everyone to another long, cold night and consuming

35

more scarce supplies. The Sturts and Lady Sale were fortunate again to have the use of Captain Johnson's tent and he gave them tea and 'Kabul cakes'. Snow was still a foot deep and even water was hard to obtain as anyone fetching it was fired on. Many died in the cold night.

Sunrise on 8 January saw disorderly scenes as an attack from the rear sent many camp followers rushing to the front that should have been controlled by the soldiers. In the process valuable ammunition was scattered and lost and a cask of spirits was opened by the artillerymen who became, as Lady Sale said, 'too much excited'. The officers managed to restore some order to parts of their corps and drove off the enemy. The artillerymen, primed with brandy, were eager to press the attack but were abused as drunkards by their commander, Captain Nicholl, who threatened to punish them! Captain Sturt soothed their indignation by praising their bravery but saying that the time for attack had not yet come. In the meantime Lady Sale and the other families had waited on horseback for several hours in the cold whilst the fighting and mayhem raged. She was grateful for: 'A tumbler of sherry, which at any other time would have made me very unlady-like, but now merely warmed me, and appeared to have no more strength in it than water. Cups full of sherry were given to young children three and four years old without in the least affecting their heads' (*Journal*, 234).

Major Thain and some of the other commanders established sufficient order amongst their men to be able to start the march at about midday but again valuable time had been lost. Elphinstone and the political agents, Major Pottinger and Captains Lawrence and Mackenzie, had been negotiating with Akbar Khan who was supposed to have protected the retreating army from attack since they left Kabul. They now agreed to what Lady Sale described as 'disgraceful propositions'. The three political agents would be taken by Akbar Khan as hostages and he was also to be given a further payment of 15,000 rupees. The army should go only as far as Tezeen until he received confirmation that General Sale had evacuated Jalalabad. Despite the fact that the British had left hostages with Akbar Khan at Kabul, paid him and the chieftains large sums of money and abandoned most of their guns as he demanded, they had received neither the supplies nor the protection that he had promised. For Elphinstone and the political agents still to believe him, delay the retreat and order General Sale to leave Jalalabad and to expose his men to the harsh winter and enemy attack was the height of folly. Sale ignored Elphinstone's orders when he received them but the retreating army had been further weakened.

Lady Sale, her daughter and son-in-law with Lieutenant Mien joined the advance guard when the army finally started moving again towards the Khoord Kabul pass but they were heavily fired on. Some Afghan chiefs rode with them and shouted to their men not to shoot but they were ignored. Major Thain's horse was found dying on the road and Sturt left his womenfolk to look for his friend and was mortally wounded in the abdomen. Lieutenant Mein and Sergeant Deane risked their lives by holding him on a pony so he slowly reached Khoord Kabul where they were camping for the night. Lady Sale had also been hit: 'I had fortunately only *one* ball *in* my arm; three others passed through my *poshteen* near the shoulder without doing me any injury. The party that fired on us was not above fifty yards from us, and we owed our escape to urging our horses on as fast as they could go' (*Journal*, 237).

Most of the military wives and their children were travelling in camel panniers and as their beasts were hit in the heavy fire they became even more vulnerable. Several women and children were snatched by Afghans, including little Mary Anderson ('Tootsey', who was to turn up unharmed several months later). Mrs Mainwaring and her baby were offered a ride by an Afghan, she wisely declined (he then stole her shawl) and walked through the snow, the dead and dying, cattle, frozen streams and rifle fire until she reached the camp still carrying her child. The rear of the army was protected by the 37th and 44th regiments who did their best to repel attacks as they entered the Khoord Kabul pass. The desperate camp followers were so intermingled with the troops and their enemies that it was difficult to fight and large numbers were killed and wounded. For a while the pass was completely blocked with struggling humanity, as the Afghan riflemen fired down on them from the heights (Illustration 12). The fingers of the soldiers of the 37th were again so frozen that they were unable to fire their weapons. By the evening Lady Sale estimated that very little ammunition remained, as much had been looted rather than fired, and that 500 soldiers and 2,500 camp followers had been killed. Of the wounded anyone with more than a slight flesh wound (such as she had) was unlikely to survive.

Captains Bygrave and Johnson again rigged up a rough tent for Lady Sale and her party and nearly thirty were packed into it. Dr Bryce examined Sturt's wound and dressed it but it was clear from his expression that there was no hope. He also cut the ball out of Lady Sale's wrist. The Sales still had Alexandrina's bedding, preserved by the *ayah*, so at least her husband had some protection during his last night. He was in 'dreadful agony' and had an 'intolerable thirst'. Lieutenant Mien constantly went with their only vessel, which was very small, to a stream to get water for him. The sepoys and camp followers around the tent were so cold that they tried to force their way in and even to get into the beds (*poshteens* spread on the snowy ground). Many more of them died during the night.

The army set off in its usual disorderly fashion on 9 January but after a mile it was ordered to halt and return to the camp. Akbar Khan was again negotiating with Elphinstone and the political agents and claimed that the arrangements for them to advance were not completed. These negotiations doomed the army to remain where they were for the whole day, only one march from where there was no snow. Sturt had been put in a camel pannier but the motion increased his sufferings and he soon died. Lady Sale and his wife took some comfort from the fact that he received a Christian burial (difficult to achieve as the Afghans often dug up the bodies of infidels). In the midst of her sorrow Lady Sale commented on the dreadful state of the army: 'More than one half the force is now frost-bitten or wounded; and most of the men can scarcely put a foot on the ground. This is the fourth day that our cattle have had no food; and the men are starved with cold and hunger' (*Journal*, 244). There were reports of more desertions.

The situation of Lady Sale and the other women, children and a few officers with accompanying wives was about to improve. Akbar Khan mendaciously promised General Elphinstone and the political agents that he would take them into his protection, treat them honourably, keep them one day's march in the rear of the army and give them a safe escort to Peshawar. He observed his first two promises but kept them all as hostages both to cow the remaining soldiers and as a guarantee for the return of his father, Dost Mohammed, to Afghanistan. Lady Sale clearly felt that she had been weak in allowing herself to be separated from the suffering army, although, with a pregnant daughter to protect, it is hard to see what else she could have done:

> Overwhelmed with domestic affliction, neither Mrs Sturt nor I were in a fit state to decide for ourselves whether we would accept the *Sirdar's* [general's] protection or not. There was but a faint hope of our ever getting safe to Jellalabad; and we followed the stream. But although there was much talk regarding our going over, all I personally know of the affair is, that I was told we were all to go, and that our horses were ready, and we must be immediately off.
>
> (*Journal*, 246).

In her defence, it was clear that the presence of women and children had provided no sort of protection to the army during the previous days. They could not have assisted the beleaguered soldiers and camp followers as they struggled towards their destruction.

The prisoners were taken to the Khoord Kabul forts where they joined others: two children, Stoker, a small boy, about three years old, whose mother had probably been killed, and Captain and Mrs Boyd's youngest son, who had been taken the previous day, and two soldier's wives. One of them, Mrs Burnes (no relation of Sir Alexander Burnes who had been murdered in Kabul), was probably called 'Mrs Bourne' (see List of Characters, Lady Sale may have mis-heard her name).They were put into three small rooms. Lady Sale's was about 14ft by 10ft and contained mother and daughter, Mrs Trevor, all her children and Mrs Smith her European servant (whose husband, a sergeant, had just been killed), Mrs Waller and a child, two soldiers' wives and little Stoker. They were given some mutton bones and greasy rice at midnight. All Lady Sale and her daughter possessed were the clothes they wore in which they had left Kabul and Lady Sale's *Journal*, which she carried on her person. The prisoners, however, were very much better off than the remainder of the army that was still attempting to retreat to Jalalabad.

The rest of Lady Sale's personal story will be reserved for later chapters but she included an account of the end of the disastrous retreat in her *Journal*. She put it together from the journals and stories of other officers who were subsequently taken prisoner. Dr Brydon also left a short account of his extraordinary survival but she did not use that.

The rest of 9 January was spent in misery for what remained of the army. Bereft of shelter, supplies and most of their animals, they were afflicted by the extreme cold and by snow blindness and more sepoys deserted. The following day, at 6.30 a.m., the 44th regiment led the advance to the Huft Kotul passes with their one remaining gun. They were unable to command the heights of the first pass, the Tunghee Tareekhee, so they had to struggle through deep snow subjected to heavy fire. The rear-guard, the 54th, were practically destroyed, although Lieutenant Henry Melville had a remarkable escape. Seeing a wounded Indian lieutenant (*jemadar*) dropping the regimental colours, he picked them up and put them under his coat. He was subsequently wounded four times and was left for dead by the Afghans but he managed to seize an abandoned pony and tried to catch up with the 44th. An Afghan horseman, who he had known in Kabul, saved him by taking him to Akbar Khan who received him kindly and arranged for his wounds to be treated.

Captain James Skinner went to Akbar Khan, who continued to tail the retreating remnants of the army. He said that he would conduct them safely to Jalalabad if they would surrender all their weapons to him. Even Elphinstone refused this unattractive offer and the march continued for 5 miles to the Tezeen *Nullah* where there were more horrific scenes of slaughter. They eventually reached the Tezeen valley, where there was no snow, at about 4.30 pm and Elphinstone decided not to rest but to press on overnight to Jugdulluk. They set off again quietly, hoping to leave the camp followers behind, but found that all those who could still stand were soon following them. They left their remaining gun behind with Dr Cardew, who had been mortally wounded at Tezeen, lying on its carriage: he died soon afterwards. The device of a night march seemed to have worked at first but eventually the rear was attacked in the bright starlight as they continued doggedly to Jugdulluk via Seh Baba. Their progress was hampered: 'by that evil that always attends Indian armies, the camp followers; who, if a shot is fired in advance, invariably fall back; and if in the rear, rush to the front, (*Journal*, 261). Brigadier Shelton, commanding a little body of soldiers in the rear, managed to hold the large force of their attackers in check (Eyre, *Military Operations at Cabul*, 240).

On the morning of 11 January the army, which had been marching for thirty hours, halted in the Jugdulluk valley on a small hill containing some ruined walls. Many had been killed by fire from the heights as they approached and they were still vulnerable to riflemen adjacent to their hill. Most of the soldiers had not eaten for days and Elphinstone managed to buy three bullocks from the camp followers that were immediately devoured raw, but it was impossible to drink from a nearby clear stream as it was in the enemy line of fire. Captain Skinner went to Akbar Khan in the late afternoon to remonstrate with him that the attacks were breaking his promises. He replied that he wished to speak directly to General Elphinstone, Brigadier Shelton and Captain Johnson who accordingly went to meet him at the top of the valley.

The British officers were hospitably treated and given good food and tea by a roaring fire but were refused permission to leave after the negotiations despite Elphinstone's protestations that it was dishonourable for him to desert his men. He was assured mendaciously that they would be given food and water early in the morning. Ominously, Akbar also said that the Ghilzai chiefs hated the British so much that the prospect of killing them was even more attractive than the money that they were being offered not to do so. Even at this late stage Elphinstone was only just beginning to realise a crucial difference between the Afghan and the British mindset. Whilst there was an expectation from the latter that once their word had been given it would be kept, Afghans were likely to regard it as positively desirable to delude foreign infidels. Loyalty to family, tribe and to Islam would supersede any other inclinations, regardless of British optimism that agreements, often accompanied by large payments of rupees, would be respected.

Fewer than a hundred active European soldiers were left by this time. They had spent the day constantly under gunfire, Captain Skinner had been treacherously killed, and the survivors were tormented by hunger and thirst. When the General did not return, they decided at 8.00 pm that their best chance was to leave. They did so, impeded as usual by the camp followers, and incurred more losses on the way, especially in a pass about 2 miles from Jugdulluk. During the confusion the few remaining cavalry officers and men seem to have ridden over the infantry (who shot at them) in the hope of making a break for Jalalabad: Brigadier Anquetil, Colonel Chambers and about twenty others were killed.

The survivors were now in more open country with little or no snow. They marched on, trying to take their wounded with them, as they knew that they would be murdered if they were left behind, but this slowed their progress. They were fired on sporadically, especially when they were near the hills. They reached the Sourkab river at 1.00 am on 13 January and several men were killed by the fire from the bridge. At dawn they could see that their enemies' numbers had grown whilst only 20 officers and 56 European soldiers remained plus about 300 camp followers. At Gandamack they made the best defensive position they could manage on a hill and there was a lull in hostilities whilst they parleyed, but after an hour the attack commenced in earnest. The Afghans were repulsed several times but the British ammunition finally ran out and all were killed except Captain Thomas Souter, who was seriously wounded, and seven or eight soldiers. The captain was probably spared because he had wrapped the regimental colours round his body and his assailants thought this dress made him an important person, worth a good ransom. These captives eventually joined Lady Sale and the others in the Laghman valley a month later. Most of the sepoys and camp followers who were not killed or did not die of their privations were taken to be sold into slavery or ended up begging on the streets of Kabul.

Dr Brydon, sometimes inaccurately described as the sole survivor of the retreat (he was actually the only European officer to reach Jalalabad), was wounded at the Jugdulluk pass. He managed to obtain a pony from a dying Hindu saddler and pressed forward with a few other horsemen to Futtehabad where they were attacked with several casualties. He was eventually separated from his other companions and after miraculously surviving another Afghan attack, reached Jalalabad where some of the defenders met him and assisted him to safety. General Sale sent out a party to look for other survivors but they only found dead bodies and Mr Baness, a Greek merchant who died a day later of tetanus and exhaustion. Over the following days a few sepoys and camp followers also made their way to Jalalabad.

Akbar Khan had attained his dual goals of destroying the main British army of occupation and of imprisoning some high-ranking officers and ladies as useful bargaining counters for the return of his father and family from India. Captain Abbott believed that he had meticulously planned the way the retreat should be managed. Akbar detained the British close to Kabul for two days because he knew that the Afghans would not attack them seriously until they were sated with plunder from the *cantonments*. He encouraged the commanders to make short marches at high altitudes where they were crippled by the intense cold and as the army entered a succession of passes Akbar arranged for fresh fighters to harry them. On the British side all was confusion and despair whereas the Afghans knew exactly what they were doing.

Could General Sale have done more to rescue the retreating army? Almost certainly, had he complied with Elphinstone's orders to evacuate Jalalabad, his whole force would have been annihilated in the passes. He lacked the men, animals and ammunition to mount a rescue expedition to Kabul (100 miles away) and by the time that he knew the fate of the few who had survived it was too late. The same option was open to General Nott at Kandahar (200 miles further away from Kabul than Jalalabad) but, wise and ruthless leader that he was, he stayed put. Neither general was prepared to put his own men at risk or lose the remaining British strategic posts in Afghanistan to rescue Elphinstone from the consequences of his own folly. Sale rightly did not allow the fact that his wife, daughter, son-in-law and unborn grandchild were at risk to weigh with him and Lady Sale held the same view:

'What are *our* lives when compared with the honour of our country?' (*Journal*, 342).

CHAPTER 4

Captivity in the Laghman Valley

The lives of the prisoners had been saved but their troubles continued as Akbar Khan regarded them as a valuable bargaining counter both with General Sale's garrison at Jalalabad and the British government that held his family in India. A powerful earthquake endangered the captives and destroyed the fortifications at Jalalabad which were, however, rapidly restored. News of relieving forces converging on Afghanistan alarmed Akbar who redoubled his efforts to conquer the force at Jalalabad or reach an agreement with them.

After the horrific events of the previous days Lady Sale and her companions now had other troubles to face. Although she did not know it, the captives were no longer in extreme physical danger. Afghan respect for upper-class women (this did not extend to the unfortunate Hindu camp followers) and Akbar Khan's wish to keep hostages for the return of his father, Dost Mohammed, and his family ensured their safety. The danger always remained, of course, that they could be assailed by hostile tribesmen or fanatical *ghazis*. There were other troubles to contend with such as travelling in the depth of winter with sick, pregnant and wounded companions (it is only later that we learn that Lady Sale's wound continued to trouble her for some time). A renowned general's wife, she seems to have been treated with some deference by the Afghans, but the whole party were entirely at the disposal of an unstable man who had been directly involved in the murder of Sir William Macnaghten. Lady Sale had a strong character and was accustomed to getting her way so her new circumstances must have been hard to bear.

Another trouble for the prisoners was the difficulty in getting accurate news, a common problem at that time, but compounded when they could take no independent action. All hell was let loose in February when Major Pottinger and Captain Macgregor (the political agent in Jalalabad) were found to be attempting to communicate secretly through a messenger. Akbar usually allowed the prisoners to write to Sale, he feared the general and wished to learn his intentions, but sometimes false news arrived even from Jalalabad. The unfortunate king Shah Shujah and his son Futteh Jung cowering in the Bala Hissar, were often misrepresented as having thrown in their lot with the rebels. The prisoners were also deluded by false reports that relief was about to arrive from Kandahar or Peshawar.

Akbar Khan knew that he had nothing left to fear from the relics of the 'army of the Indus'. Most were dead and he held some officers and their wives and ordinary soldiers as prisoners; thousands of sepoys and camp followers were sold into slavery, were dying a slow, cruel death in the freezing passes or ended up in Kabul supported by charitable Afghans and Hindus. Captain Abbott heard in Jalalabad that: 'Our Sepoys return to Cabul in great numbers, in a sad state from the cold. The camp-followers are sold in the bazaar for one rupee each' (Abbott, 266). Akbar continued to worry about the remaining British garrisons in Ghazni, Kalat-i-Ghilzai, Kandahar and Jalalabad. He knew that the latter two towns could be used as bases for the reconquest of Kabul from Quetta and Peshawar and that in the spring the British army was likely to relieve them both. He had tried to dislodge Sale through the attacks of local tribesmen and failed, he had included the evacuation of Jalalabad in all his treaty demands but 'Fighting Bob' had stayed put. Akbar's strategy was to keep the hostages in the vicinity of Jalalabad but not near enough for them to be rescued and, if all else failed, make an attack on the town when the weather improved.

During their first months of captivity most of the prisoners, apart from the sick and wounded in Kabul, were brought together in one place. Initially, on the afternoon of 13 January, at Khoord Kabul, the women and children and their husbands were joined by General Elphinstone and his fellow officers who had been treacherously captured by Akbar Khan. Lieutenant Melville (see Part I, Chapter 3) and Mr Mcgrath, a surgeon,

45

both of them wounded, also arrived. Given the state of many of the prisoners and the fact that several ladies were pregnant, the arrival of a medical man, even a wounded one, was timely before they started an arduous journey. They were conducted by Sultan Jan, a cousin of Akbar Khan, who led a body of about 600 Afghan cavalry and irregular horse, some had formerly been employed by the British but had deserted. The Europeans rode on horseback with some of the women and children (but not Lady Sale and her daughter) in camel panniers, passing over the mountains to the Laghman valley.

The journey commenced on the following day; they travelled over rough and precipitous roads but managed to cover 24 miles to Kutz-i-Mahomed Ali Khan. Lady Sale gave a vivid account of the terrain: at Adrak-Budrak pass she had to hold onto the mane of her horse (and her wounded wrist was still troubling her) fearing that she and her saddle would slip off into the abyss as she had no groom (*sace*) to help her. She admired the wild, romantic scenery but encountered other distressing and less elevating sights:

> At the commencement of the defile, and for some considerable distance, we passed 200 or 300 of our miserable Hindostanees, who had escaped up the unfrequented road from the massacre of the 12th. They were all naked, and more or less frostbitten: wounded, and starving, they had set fire to the bushes and grass, and huddled all together to impart warmth to each other. Subsequently we heard that scarcely any of these poor wretches escaped from the defile: and that driven to the extreme of hunger they had sustained life by feeding on their dead comrades.
>
> (*Journal*, 281)

The party bivouacked by a fort since the occupants would not admit the infidels (*kaffirs*) so they slept outside rolled in their *poshteens* with saddles for pillows. Elphinstone, Shelton and Johnson were allowed into a cowshed where they enjoyed a blazing fire. Later these officers and Melville (for whom, together with Bygrave, Akbar Khan seems to have had a particular liking) were invited into the fort for tea, a good dinner and a warm night's rest. Lady Sale probably showed great restraint in expressing no irritation at their good fortune.

They were off to an early start the next day to cross the two branches of the fast flowing Panjshir river. Lady Sale and the others were helped across by Akbar and the chiefs; as it was five people (presumably Afghans) were swept away. The prisoners were pleased to see that a great number of troublesome camp dogs, who had followed them since their masters had died, were unable to pass the torrent. They travelled 20 miles over barren country and passed Kubber-i-Lamach, a celebrated place of pilgrimage to the tomb of the reputed father of Noah. They arrived at 3.00 pm at the fortified town of Tigri where Elphinstone and the other senior officers stayed with Akbar and the rest were housed in the fort of another chief. He did his best to offer Lady Sale hospitality, taking her and her daughter to visit his mother and wife. They received them kindly and gave them a large sweetmeat made of brown sugar and pistachio nuts: a welcome change from the coarse food that was their staple diet.

The following day was a Sunday and the Europeans rested in the fort. They read from a Bible and prayer book that had been picked up on the bloody field of Boothak: Captains Mackenzie and Johnson were to conduct services regularly on Sundays. Lady Sale did not express religious sentiments in her *Journal* unlike many of her contemporaries and the clergyman, Isaac Allen, whose *Diary* is the subject of the second part of this book. She appears to have been a conventional Christian and, whatever her private thoughts, would have believed religious observances to have been good for British discipline and morale. By this time she was writing for a wider audience than just her husband and this would have conditioned the language that she used. The fort was attacked during the day by tribesmen who had a feud with the owner but, apart from a few shots and much shouting, nothing happened: an everyday story of Afghan life.

On 17 January they were on the move again, riding up the Laghman valley away from Jalalabad; Akbar was alarmed by the hostility of the locals to his prisoners and had to resume the journey for their own safety. They thus lost any hope that they would soon be free: 'We plainly saw that, whatever might be said, we were virtually prisoners, until such time as Sale shall evacuate Jellalabad, or the Dost be permitted by our government to return to this country' (*Journal*, 284).

Akbar was still hoping that Pottinger could prevail upon Sale to leave Jalalabad, although Pottinger pointed out that, as he was a prisoner, he had no authority over other British soldiers or political agents (Eyre, *Military Operations at Cabul*, 271). They rode 8 or 9 miles almost to the top of the valley, close to the first range of hills towards Kaffiristan, to Buddeabad: although they did not realise it, this was to be their 'home' for some time. They were lodged in the largest fort in an inner square or citadel, the few European soldiers who had survived were placed in a cellar (*tykana*), the remainder of the prisoners were put in rooms above. On that day they were horrified to learn that only Dr Brydon had managed to reach Jalalabad alive from the retreat through the passes. This bore out what Lady Sale had been told in Kabul: 'that Mohammed Akbar would annihilate the whole army, except one man, who would reach Jellalabad to tell the tale' (*Journal*, 285).

The fort belonged to Mohammed Shah Khan, a Ghilzai chief who was one of Akbar's fathers-in-law and was used by Mohammed and his favourite wife. His brother Dost Mohammed Khan was given charge of the prisoners with a secretary (*mirza*) seeing to their daily needs. The officers and ladies were allocated six rooms (two soldiers' wives and the little boy, Stoker, were in the airless cellar with the other ranks). Lady Macnaghten, Captain and Mrs Anderson and their remaining two children, Captain and Mrs Boyd (she gave birth to a daughter on 14 March) and their two children, Mrs Mainwaring (her husband was with Sale in Jalalabad) and one child, the Eyres', and a girl, Hester Macdonald, were in one room. The adjoining room was 'appropriated' for their servants and baggage. Captain Mackenzie and his Christian servant from Madras, Jacob, Mr Riley (a conductor of ordnance), his wife and their two children and Mr Fallon (a clerk) occupied another room. Mrs Trevor, her seven children and servant Mrs Smith, Lieutenant and Mrs Waller and their child, Lieutenant Mien, Mrs Sturt and Lady Sale had another room. She does not tell us where her Hindu servants were accommodated but we know she had some. All the rest of the officers, including General Elphinstone, were 'crammed' into the two remaining rooms.

In a status-conscious society it must have been very trying for the senior wives to be in such close proximity to men who were not their husbands and even to servants, but Lady Sale seems to have made the best of it with grim humour: 'It did not take us much time to arrange our property; consisting of a mattress and *resai* [quilt] between us, and no clothes except those we had on, and in which we left Cabul' (*Journal*, 286). Mackenzie records that that the gentlemen who shared rooms with ladies observed the greatest propriety and 'cleared out' early each morning to allow them some privacy. He also criticised some of the ladies for giving themselves airs as officers' wives in front of Mrs Riley, a 'very superior' person.

The prisoners were visited by Akbar Khan who mendaciously assured them that they were not prisoners and that they would be escorted to Jalalabad. He also offered to forward a letter to General Sale and his wife wrote a few 'guarded words' assuring him that she and their daughter were safe and well. On 19 January they were able to wash for the first time since leaving Kabul, although Lady Sale found that it was a painful process as the cold and the glare of the sun had peeled her face of skin. They appreciated their breakfast of hot radishes and lentils, a welcome addition to their staple diet of lamb, rice and coarse *chappaties*. This was made even more unpalatable to the Europeans by the Afghan cooks' practice of dousing it with rancid melted butter (*ghee*): at least everyone got a fair share as Captain Lawrence was in charge of portion control. Eyre reported that they eventually arranged that their own servants could cook the food in a fashion more suited to British stomachs.

A letter arrived from Sale on 22 January that had only been written three days previously. He said that they could hold out at Jalalabad for six months, that Brigadier Wild would be arriving there from Peshawar immediately and that General Pollock was making his way across the Punjab with an army. He probably wrote all this as much for Akbar's ears as for his wife: an elaborate game of bluff and counter bluff was going on and the Jalalabad garrison played it rather well. The following day Akbar visited the prisoners and took another letter to be sent to Sale. He also said, falsely, that Shah Shujah wanted to be given four British officers so he could put them to death: the *Sirdar* had everything to gain from fostering divisions between the old king and the Europeans.

Akbar certainly had nothing to fear from Brigadier Wild, that unfortunate officer had been languishing at Peshawar with inadequate men, guns and supplies even to relieve the little fort at the entrance of the Khyber pass, Ali Musjid, let alone Jalalabad. By the end of January, after several fiascos, Ali Musjid was abandoned by the British and they could do nothing but wait for General Pollock. The Sikhs were in disarray after the death of Ranjit Singh and their troops, sent to Wild in accordance with the treaty, scared the sepoys with tales of the impregnability of the Khyber and eventually mutinied and returned home. Meanwhile, General Nott at Kandahhar fumed at the lack of support for his hungry garrison which, like General Sale, lacked adequate ammunition and treasure.

In practical respects the situation of the prisoners continued to improve: Akbar gave the ladies gifts of cloth (some they suspected had been looted from their retreating army) so they could make new outfits and 1,000 rupees to be divided amongst all the prisoners. Dost Mohammed Khan took Mrs Trevor's boys and some of the officers walking in the sugarcane fields near the fort which they greatly enjoyed. It is clear, however, from her *Journal* that Lady Sale and the other ladies never went out until the party left the fort. This would not have been deliberate cruelty on the part of their captors, but arose out of the Afghans' feeling that the proper place for high-class women was indoors.

General Sale sent Lady Sale her chest of drawers, which miraculously had not been opened, on 27 January together with a letter. On 10 February he sent his wife and daughter some boxes containing useful items and, to their joy, books. They also contained a number of needles but all Captain Mackenzie's diplomacy failed to obtain any of them for the other ladies who were in great need. Conversely, young Mrs Mainwaring received a box of useful articles from her husband and liberally distributed its contents among the other ladies (Mackenzie, vol. 1, 281–2). On the same day they were joined by additional prisoners, Major Charles Griffiths and Mr F.C. Blewitt, a clerk. They owed their lives to the fact that on 13 January they had left the embattled little force at Gandamack to negotiate at a nearby fort during a pause in the fighting. Mr Blewitt spoke Persian and was to act as an interpreter but, whilst they were absent, the force was annihilated and they were taken into protective custody by a chief. Several European soldiers had been taken alive and also Captain Thomas Souter, who was severely wounded. One of this group, Sergeant Major Lisson, had been allowed to go to Jalalabad to explain the situation to Sale: the Afghans probably hoped the awful news would encourage him to surrender. Lisson was accompanied by an Afghan who was content to receive a ransom of 500 rupees to leave him there. When Akbar Khan heard the news that these captives had been taken he insisted that they should be sent to him, apart from Souter who was too ill to travel.

On 14 February all the officers had to surrender their arms to their captors, a punishment for the clandestine correspondence between Pottinger and Captain Macgregor at Jalalabad: 'I took poor Sturt's sword myself and begged that the *Sirdar* would keep it himself; that we might be sure of its restoration, as being valuable to his widow. Dost Mohammed Khan . . . desired me to keep it myself; acting in the handsomest manner, and evincing much feeling on the occasion' (*Journal*, 294). The servants were not so fortunate: under the pretext of a general search, all their remaining money was taken.

Akbar Khan was making another attempt to secure the surrender of Jalalabad. Probably under compulsion Shah Shuja wrote ordering the garrison to vacate it and return to Peshawar. Most of the officers in council, including Sale and Macgregor, were inclined to obey him and trust the promises of a peaceful, protected retreat. Captain Broadfoot, almost single-handed, resisted the Afghan blandishments pointing out the dangers of a winter retreat and reminding the council of the fate of Elphinstone's force that had withdrawn from Kabul after a treaty had been signed with Akbar and the chiefs. On 13 February news arrived that British forces really were moving to their relief through the Punjab and this tipped the argument in favour of Broadfoot and of staying put in Jalalabad. Lady Sale had heard about the letter from the king but she did not know at that time how close her husband had been to retreating. Later the British government did all it could to disguise that fact but the assiduous work of Kaye had uncovered the relevant documents by the mid-1850s (Kaye, vol. 3, 55–65).

The prisoners believed that Akbar Khan had started an assault on Jalalabad, as in the following days they could hear gunfire and all sorts of rumours reached them about what was happening. In fact, the *Sirdar* seemed reluctant to attack the town and was content to try and blockade it for the time being; this only led to minor skirmishes but the garrison was getting short of food. They did, however, club together to send the officers at Buddeabad some extra clothes and Lady Sale was delighted to receive a packet of letters from friends and family in India and England as well as a letter from her husband. The officers at Jalalabad and the prisoners had devised a simple way of communicating without the Afghans' knowledge: the former dotted certain letters of the alphabet in the newspapers they sent to make sentences.

A major earthquake struck the Laghman valley and Jalalabad on 19 February, destroying most of Broadfoot's carefully constructed fortifications and wrecking even the Spartan living conditions of the captives. Lady Sale was on the roof over their room collecting her laundry when it started but she managed to climb down, fearing that it would collapse and that her daughter would be buried. To her relief everyone had escaped into the courtyard and no one was injured: even Lady Macnaghten's beloved cat was dug out of the ruins unscathed. (This cat led a chequered existence – the rascally gaoler had twice kidnapped it and exacted a ransom of 20 rupees for its return). Mackenzie was also sitting on the roof at the time with Brigadier Shelton and they rushed down to safety. That evening Shelton (who had quarrelled with practically all the prisoners) said solemnly to him: "'Mackenzie, you went down stairs *first* today". He coolly replied: "It's the fashion in an earthquake, Brigadier. I learnt it among the Spaniards in Manilla'"(Mackenzie, vol. 1, 284–5).

There were at least twenty-five after-shocks before dark and they continued for the next few days but with diminishing severity. The officers gave up one of their rooms to Lady Sale's group as her's had lost its roof and most of the Europeans preferred to sleep in the courtyard despite the cold and damp. Dost Mohammed Khan, when he brought workmen to clear the debris, told them that their fort had sustained less damage than many others in the valley where several people had been killed. Lady Sale wrote to her husband to assure him that they were all safe but received alarming reports that the defences of Jalalabad had been destroyed and the town had been taken.

Captain Bulstrode Bygrave arrived at Buddeabad on 23 February and was received with delight as it had been supposed that he was dead. He had escaped the carnage on 12 January and hidden in the mountains for seven days but sustained severe frostbite, losing all the toes on one foot. He was accompanied by Mr Baness the merchant, they shared a small bag of coffee grains and found wild liquorice root growing in the Sourkab river. Since Bygrave could only move very slowly, Baness reluctantly went on alone to Jalalabad where he soon died. Bygrave had, in the meantime, surrendered to a chief in a village only 4 miles from Gandamack who was forced to send him to Akbar Khan.

The following days at the fort were troubled with constant little earthquakes and all sorts of news, much of it false, about Jalalabad. The industrious Broadfoot quickly repaired its defences leading a healthy and motivated work force improved, cynics suggested, by the fact that the rum supply had run out. The garrison's resolute resistance seems to have hardened Akbar's heart against the hostages. On 28 February he ordered that their guards should be doubled and a few days later all their servants, who were frostbitten and unable to work, were sent out of the fort after being robbed of all they possessed. The *mirza* and Captain Lawrence, however, later managed to secure the return of some who were still in the vicinity. On 9 March there was a great rumpus when a Hindu sweeper endeavoured to strangle Lady Sale's *ayah* in a jealous rage. He was flogged and would have been hanged but for the intervention of the officers, but he received the almost equally deadly punishment of being stripped and sent out into the cold.

The earthquakes continued as did the arrival of news from Jalalabad. It was clear from the number of wounded Afghans coming to Buddeabad that Sale's garrison was getting the best of the conflict. They had thwarted an attempt to mine the walls by Broadfoot's prompt action and Akbar Khan, who had already been injured, received two more wounds. Various tales were told to explain how this happened: Shah Shujah had bribed an assassin; Macgregor had paid Akbar's cousin to kill him; it was an accident. In any case, it meant that at a time critical to his survival, the *Sirdar* was incapacitated. It was probably a sign of his weakening situation that led Akbar to contemplate separating the single officers from the married women and their children. When Captain Lawrence expostulated with the *Sirdar*, Mahommed Shah Khan ranted at him: 'as long as there is an

Affghan prisoner in India, or a *Feringhee* soldier in Affghanistan, so long we will retain you, men, women, and children. When you can ride you *shall* ride, when you cannot ride you *shall* walk, when you cannot walk you *shall* be dragged, and when you cannot be dragged *your throats shall be cut*' (Lawrence, 188). Lawrence shamed him by saying that warriors should not speak like that to men who were prisoners, Akbar assured the officer that he did not mean it and Mahommed Shah Khan followed him, as he swept out, with an apology and the prisoners stayed together.

Farriers came to shoe the Europeans' horses, making them think that their departure was imminent. They had made themselves a little more comfortable: those who continued to sleep in the courtyard had paid for two temporary sheds to be erected. Lady Sale and her daughter preferred to remain in the upper room, its roof shored up with a prop. They had acquired stools, a rough table and *charpoys* (beds with four poles and ropes crossed over them). Some of the prisoners still had money that enabled them to purchase such comforts and, later, even ponies for their journey. The *mirza* who had been their deputy gaoler had been replaced by Dost Mohammed Khan's steward (*nazir*). He started well by increasing the prisoners' daily allowance to two sheep and twenty fowls between them and one *seer* (about 2lb) of flour and one of rice and *ghee* to each room and monthly supplies of raisins, tea and sugar. On 21 March Melville cheered the ladies up by bringing them a bouquet of narcissi, the first green things they had seen for a long time. But they were still receiving misleading reports about Jalalabad, for example, that a British relieving force had arrived there. The sceptical Lady Sale observed: 'All the forts about this place are filling fast with wounded men of Akbar's army; and skirmishes are said to take place daily at Jellalabad, in which we never hear of the *Sirdar* being victorious' (*Journal*, 310).

The prisoners in Buddeabad continued to be troubled by small earthquakes and by conflicting accounts of the military situation up to and beyond Easter Sunday (27 March). One minute they heard that they were all to be sold as slaves at Bokhara, the next that they were to be freed and sent to Jalalabad. They noticed that the Afghans were treating them more respectfully as Pollock's army approached. Some asked if the British would spare their lives to which they replied: 'all who behave well to us will have their property respected, and be well treated' (*Journal*, 314).

On 6 April two disturbing pieces of news arrived: the garrison at Ghazni led by Colonel Palmer had surrendered and the officers who survived were captives but most of the soldiers had either been killed or sold into slavery. The prisoners also heard that Shah Shujah had been murdered by the son of Shah Zeman Khan when he was tempted to leave the Bala Hissar to head the chiefs who were marching on Jalalabad. Both these reports subsequently proved to be accurate, although the prisoners were also told that the officers from Ghazni were being well treated: in fact they were harshly used and Colonel Palmer was tortured. Shah Shujah's son, Futteh Jung, continued to hold out in the Bala Hissar and to enjoy the support of some of the local chiefs, to the intense annoyance of Akbar Khan and his allies.

The prisoners received many misleading reports of what was going on at Jalalabad but on 7 April the garrison really did attack Akbar Khan and gained a decisive victory. His greatly superior force was routed, his camp destroyed and four guns, lost by the British at Kabul and Gandamack, were recaptured. The British had been able to fight on fairly level ground where their superior discipline and fire-power counted. Captain Abbott deployed his artillery to great effect, a sepoy once said of him: 'He is such a shot that if you set up a needle, Abbott Sahib will send a ball through its eye' (Low, 310). Colonel Dennie was killed in the early stages of the battle but British losses only amounted to ten dead and fifty-three wounded. The result for the British prisoners, however, was not so good.

The Afghan chiefs had always quarrelled among themselves and the defeat of Akbar Khan undermined his authority over them. He was falling back on Kabul for a last stand against the British and wished to ensure that the prisoners were not liberated, taken by one of the rival chiefs or massacred by the fanatical *ghazis*. This meant that it was time for them to quit the Laghman valley and on 10 April they were summarily ordered to pack and leave. Mohammed Shah Khan had, up to then, behaved fairly decently towards them but suddenly he and his servants showed an avaricious side. He took all Lady Macnaghten's valuable jewels and her

55

shawls that were worth 30–40,000 rupees. Lady Sale had to abandon a large box that she could not carry and was also deprived of her chest of drawers, but hoped to take her revenge on the pillagers: 'I left some rubbish in them, and some small bottles, that were useless to me. I hope the Affghans try their contents as medicine, and find them efficacious: one bottle contained nitric acid, another a strong solution of lunar caustic!' (*Journal*, 319).

The prisoners finally started on their journey after noon but there were still delays: Mrs Sturt's camel broke down and she was given a horse by the chivalrous Lieutenant Melville. Unfortunately, the *mirza*, who had reappeared to obtain any pickings he could get, offered to look after the valuable fur-lined cloak and sword which had belonged to the late husband of Alexandrina Sturt and Lady Sale said that she never saw them again. Captain Lawrence, however, reported on 16 September when the prisoners left Bamian to return to Kabul, that she trusted the sword to his keeping saying that: 'it was in safe hands, and would be well used if needed' (Lawrence, 222). Presumably she overlooked the entry in her *Journal* that she had written at the time and did not correct it before publication. The party had only gone a short distance when they were told to turn round and return to Mohammed Shah Khan's fort at Buddeabad. They found that everything had been taken away during their brief absence, even the huts in the courtyard. But they were told not to unpack as they would soon be leaving again and were glad to be given some cooked chickens as the unaccustomed exercise had made them very hungry.

There had been much talk of ransoming the prisoners in previous weeks and Akbar Khan and the generals in Kandahar and Jalalabad could have done a deal to effect their release and save them from further months of suffering and anxiety. Unfortunately, it was impossible to trust Akbar Khan who had broken his word many times and, from his point of view, he was not yet ready to accept that he had been defeated; he also knew that in the prisoners he had a valuable diplomatic resource. As the Duke of Wellington observed in March: 'the captivity of the women would produce an effect from one end of Asia to the other, such as Europeans could form no idea of' (Norris, 396).

CHAPTER 5

Back to Kabul

The appearance of General Pollock at Jalalabad in mid-April 1842 and General England at Kandahar two weeks later changed the situation for the prisoners. Akbar Khan started to negotiate for their release only to find he was offered nothing in return, for the British did not trust him. His only resort was to drag his prisoners with him to Kabul whilst he resisted the armies with his chieftain allies and struggled to dislodge Shah Shujah's son, Futteh Jung, from the Bala Hissar.

Despite the reverses of the previous day, the prisoners got off to an early start after breakfast on 11 April 1842. The European soldiers were left behind with the two wives, 'Mrs Burnes' and Mrs Wade, the child Seymour Stoker, the injured servants and those who did not wish to go. Lady Sale believed that, 'the women and child certainly ought to have accompanied us'. This proved to be true since, when the main party left, Mrs Wade the half-Asian wife of a sergeant, adopted the local costume, proclaimed that she was a Muslim and took an Afghan lover. She compounded this shocking behaviour by telling her new friends about the British soldiers' plans to escape, which nearly resulted in their throats being cut, and about the gold coins her husband had hidden in his boots. Worst of all she took little Stoker with her when she joined her lover and, according to Mackenzie, treated him so badly that he died.

The prisoners travelled a long way past many forts destroyed by the earthquake, and arrived at Ali Kund where they all had to squeeze into three tents. Akbar Khan was there seated in a palanquin and looking very sick: 'He was particular in bowing to us all, making every demonstration of civility' (*Journal*, 321). After the long weeks of confinement in a fort, Lady Sale revelled in the beauty of the countryside and especially in the flowers:

sweet pea, cranesbill, gentian, forget-me-not and campion. Akbar's cousin, Sultan Jan, a handsome, boastful man, arrived at their camp looking miserable after his defeat by Pollock's forces at the Khyber. On 5 April British soldiers, including Gurkha hillmen, had crowned the heights at the entry to the pass, rendering the barrier that had been erected across it useless. Only 50 men remained of the 500 Sultan Jan had taken with him and he had been burned black by his exposure to the elements. Lady Sale remarked that sunburn made the Europeans look like Afghans and the Afghans look like Hindus.

On 12 April the prisoners made an unpleasant journey through a parched country where the scanty pools were too shallow and sandy for their horses to drink and they also had to ride up and down some very difficult mountain passes. The following day they travelled for 12 miles through equally sterile country. Lady Sale always rode her horse but, on one awkward ascent, the ladies in camel panniers had to get out and make the ascent on foot. As they were camping they used tents, which were very hot, everyone stayed each night in their allocated place but found the cramped conditions extremely trying.

The party had to climb a difficult hill on 14 April but found the sight of fruit trees in blossom and Mohammed Shah Khan's sons carrying bouquets of tulips cheering. They crossed and re-crossed the same stream but when they reached the Kabul river they used a raft and camped on the bank with Akbar Khan, amusing themselves by watching some of his horses and riders battling through the rapid current. The party remained there until the middle of the following day when they only progressed 5 miles to Sehruby. No camel panniers were available so there was 'great grumbling' amongst the ladies. They were, however, pleased by the sight of amaryllis in bloom and by the sweet scent of the Persian iris. Less pleasing was an especially distressing rumour (untrue) that all the hostages left in Kabul had been murdered. Rumours persisted during the following three days when they stayed in the same place: Shah Shujah had not been murdered and was ruling in Kabul; the prisoners were to join other British officers at Tezeen; everyone was to walk to Herat after which they were to be sent to Balkh.

The arrival at Jalalabad of General Pollock with a large force and supplies on 15 April was probably the source of much of the frenetic chattering by the Afghans, although it would be some time before the prisoners were sure that Sale had been reinforced. Jalalabad after Akbar's army had besieged it and denuded the surrounding countryside of food and fodder was, 'one of the most miserable-looking places I ever beheld' (Greenwood, 121), but Pollock, despite Afghan fears, was to remain there for several months. So strong were the British in the area that they were able to find sufficient provisions and forage for the approximately 10,000 soldiers and 50,000 camp followers that the conjunction of Sale's and Pollock's forces produced.

During the pause of several days Lady Sale, who had withstood the effects of her wound and many privations, succumbed to a high fever. They travelled through heavy rain to Tezeen on 19 April and she was too weak from the fever to ride so Akbar Khan lent his palanquin to her and Lady Macnaghten but: 'as I had to sit backwards, with very little room, nothing to lean against, and to keep a balance against Lady M. and Mrs Boyd's baby, I benefited but little except in the grandeur of a royal equipage. My turban and habit were completely saturated by the rain; and I shivered as I went' (*Journal*, 326).

At Tezeen they were lodged in a fort that had been damaged by the earthquake. The women were kindly received by the chief's ladies who stoked up three fires to dry their clothes (unsuccessfully because Victorian women wore a great deal). Their bedding was also sopping wet and Lady Sale's fever heightened her discomfort. This was not improved by the offer of a dinner of rice topped by sour curds and *ghee*, although she did manage to get some tea that was more acceptable. They lay down to sleep on mats as their bedding was unusable, thirty-four in a room that measured 15ft by 12ft with a fire in the centre. Lady Sale started shivering but was rescued by Captain Anderson who covered her with a bed cloak that soon warmed her.

'The *Sirdar* fears that if he is taken by us we shall either hang him or blow him from a gun' (*Journal*, 327). Perhaps that was why, on 20 April, there was a rumour that Captain Mackenzie was to go to Jalalabad on a secret mission to treat with Pollock, although he did not, in fact, depart until a few days later.

Mrs Waller gave birth to a daughter, who her parents named Tezeena, and was given a room with just her family and Lieutenant and Mrs Eyre and their child so only twenty-nine had to sleep in the original room. The following day they were sent out of the fort into the rain but only went a mile. General Elphinstone, who was dying, Dr Mcgrath, the political agents, Pottinger and Mackenzie, the Wallers and the Eyres were left in the fort.

> Major Pottinger expostulated with Akbar; and told him that surely he did not make war on women and children, and that it was great cruelty to drive us about the country in the way they are doing; that when the Dost and the ladies of his family [amongst them Akbar's wives] went to Hindostan they travelled with every comfort procurable, and probably many more than they would have experienced in their own country.
>
> (*Journal*, 328–9)

Akbar protested that he could do nothing until Mohammed Shah Khan returned from Kabul and that his father in India was closely guarded. Pottinger, who was clearly angry, replied that the Dost was allowed to go out hawking whenever he wished and, if he had an escort of horse, it was only what his high rank required. Any restraint placed upon his womenfolk was what he himself had desired: the exchange makes it clear why Akbar disliked the plain-speaking Pottinger.

Despite Pottinger's expostulations, Akbar, who feared that other leaders were intent upon seizing his prisoners, put them through another difficult journey on 22 April. Lady Sale was still too weak to ride but Mrs Boyd gave up her place in a small camel pannier, which, however, seems to have been even more uncomfortable than the palanquin. Lady Sale was holding Mrs Boyd's baby and found that she only had a space of 1½ft square in which to double up her long legs: she vowed that she would rather walk than ride in another camel pannier. They travelled for about 12 miles up the bed of a deep ravine, passing caves containing the distressing sight of dead and dying camp followers from the January retreat.

The prisoners were in the heart of Ghilzai territory, the Jubher Khail country above the Tezeen valley, and there was still ice and snow on the ground. Their Afghan captors were interested in the very different political arrangements that existed in Britain. At a dinner for Mrs Eyre, for example, Mohamed Shah Khan's ladies were astonished to learn that her country was governed by a woman. Having heard that Lieutenant Eyre was an artist, Akbar sent for him and, despite his religion, asked the officer to draw one of his followers and a favourite horse. He also questioned Eyre a great deal about 'artillery matters' and asked to be shown how to use a sextant. As it was broken he asked Eyre to remove the coloured glass from it so he could make sunglasses! (Eyre, *Military Operations at Cabul*, 300–2).

The group were glad to hear that they would be staying at their new camp for over a week and their horses were sent back to Tezeen as they could not be fed in the hills. Lady Sale's was saved from the Afghans (the horses disappeared and were later replaced by ponies) by the fortunate chance that it was given to Captain Mackenzie when he departed on his mission from Akbar to Jalalabad. Whilst it was there it went lame so it did not return to Tezeen. The chiefs were unwilling to allow a British officer to go to Jalalabad fearing that he would not return. Eventually, on 23 April: 'they all pitched upon me, for they had got it into their heads that I was a Mullah, and they thought that I would come back' (Mackenzie, vol. 1, 317). Their belief probably arose from the religious services that Mackenzie and Johnson conducted every Sunday. The chiefs warned Mackenzie, however, of the dangers of the journey: his apprehensions were not improved by them entrusting him to the guardianship of Batti Dusd, 'Batti the Thief'. He had taken hundreds of camels from Sale on his march to Jalalabad and then sold them back to him (see Part I, Chapter 1). Batti turned out to be a resourceful guide who led Mackenzie by devious routes, avoiding at least some of the wild tribesmen who would have killed the *feringhee* if they had penetrated his disguise, for he habitually now dressed as an Afghan (Illustration 9). He gained a great reputation amongst the chiefs for going to Jalalabad and then, according to his word, for returning to Akbar Khan and repeating the dangerous journey in May.

General Elphinstone died of his illnesses on 23 April whilst he and the others who had stayed behind in the fort were being hurried away after a rumour that it was to be attacked. Akbar sent his body back to Jalalabad escorted by nine Afghans and Private Miller, who had served the General with devotion, disguised as an Afghan. They were stopped near Jugdulluk by tribesmen who thought that the box contained treasure. When they discovered their mistake they stoned the body and Miller was beaten and knifed, he saved his life by swearing that he was a Muslim. Akbar Khan was mortified that his gesture had misfired and again the General's corpse was sent on to Jalalabad and buried with full military honours, but Miller had to rejoin the other prisoners. The European soldiers in Kabul, the sick and wounded who had been left behind in January, were reported to have been sent to Loghur, the country of a particularly nasty chieftain.

Meanwhile, the pause in their travels and better weather improved conditions for the prisoners. They made sun shelters out of their bedding during the daytime and later covered them with juniper. Food, however, was in short supply as Akbar had run out of money and could not even give his own troops adequate pay, although the Europeans were able to secure some flour and twelve sheep. Rumours, more or less alarming, continued to fly around but on 3 May Lady Sale received a letter from her husband so she would have had some inkling of what was happening. She also heard that the Kabul chiefs were at each others' throats, united only in their hatred of Akbar Khan for bringing the British back in force to Afghanistan. He feared to go to Kabul in case he was assassinated and his shortage of money effectively put him under the control of his father-in-law Mohammed Shah Khan. At this stage he seemed to get on better with brave and intelligent men like Mackenzie, Eyre and Bygrave than with his own people. When some of the British officers were escorted to go shooting in the hills, they could hear the sound of gunfire from Kabul which was about 30 miles away. Meanwhile, General Pollock had proclaimed that all Afghans who remained quiet would not be molested.

The Wallers, Eyres and others who had remained behind at the Tezeen fort rejoined the main party of prisoners on 3 May. The weather continued to improve, although it was still cold enough at the tents in the mornings to cover the *beesties'* (water carriers) buckets with ice. The recently widowed wife of Sergeant Deane (who had helped Captain Sturt, see Part I, Chapter 3), a very pretty Persian woman, was forcibly married to the younger brother of Mohammed Shah Khan: 'Whenever this man enters her presence, she salutes him with her slipper' (*Journal*, 341). More cheerfully young Mary Anderson ('Tootsey') was restored to her parents on 10 May. She had been offered for sale through the streets of Kabul for 4,000 rupees but by the good offices of one of the hostages, Lieutenant Conolly, had been taken under the protection of the kindly and moderate Zeman Shah Khan. She had been taught to say: 'My father and mother are infidels, but I am a Mussulman' (Eyre, *Military Operations at Cabul*, 312).

The fighting amongst the chiefs in Kabul continued and Lady Sale believed that the citizens, whose businesses were suffering, would welcome the return of the British. Her assessment of the situation was characteristically robust:

> Now is the time to strike the blow, but I much dread dilly-dallying just because a handful of us are in Akbar's power. What are our lives when compared with the honour of our country? Not that I am at all inclined to have my throat cut: on the contrary I hope that I shall live to see the British flag once more triumphant in Affghanistan; and then I have no objection to the Ameer Dost Mahommed Khan being reinstated: only let us first show them that we can conquer them, and humble their treacherous chiefs in the dust.
>
> (*Journal*, 342)

The main concern of Ellenborough seems, in fact, not to have been the safety of the prisoners but the fear of another humiliating defeat. That fear was to keep the relieving forces in Kandahar and Jalalabad for three more months and without the impact on public opinion of the letters and *Journal* of Lady Sale which were published in the Indian and British papers and the upbeat reports of Generals Pollock and Nott, they might never have moved forward.

Spasmodic negotiations to ransom the prisoners did continue but they seem to have realised that they would remain in captivity for some time. They heard that the Hindu servants whom they had left at Buddeabad had been turned out of the fort again after being stripped of their clothing.

Those who were in reasonable condition had been sold as slaves, the men for 46 rupees each, the women for 22. Endless reports continued to reach the prisoners about the progress of the British forces at Kandahar and Jalalabad and about who had most power in Kabul. Their captors continued to feed them as much false information as possible and to punish any unauthorised attempts to get news.

An Afghan gentleman sent Lady Sale and her daughter some tea and sugar, a kind attention that was much appreciated. On her wedding anniversary, 16 May, she and her daughter dined with the ladies of Mohamed Shah Khan's family, using two female servants as interpreters. They ate pillau and sour and sweet curd from a very dirty cloth spread on the carpet. The Afghan ladies, according to etiquette, did not eat with the infidels (*kaffirs*) but were 'profuse in their expressions of good will'. Lady Sale was unimpressed with the appearance of these ladies: 'most were fat and wore robes of poor quality, resembling common night-dresses. The favourite wore gold coins as ornaments but the rest only had silver and a few jewels: About seven common-sized pearls surrounding an emerald full of flaws, the whole set as a nose ornament, was the handsomest thing I saw in the trinket way' (*Journal*, 346). The ladies wore their hair in many small plaits, well stiffened with gum. More generally, Lady Sale observed that the women of Kabul liked to use red and white paint and decorate their hands and wrists so they looked as if they had been plunged in blood. When they went out they wore the *burka*, a veil, leg wraps and high-heeled iron-shod slippers.

In the evening of 16 May Mackenzie arrived with a letter from Sale that updated his wife on the movements of Pollock and England: the former could not go forward until he received orders from Ellenborough. She was irritated by such hesitation believing that their forces could easily march to Kabul and defeat Akbar Khan. She learnt from Mackenzie that Sale had fallen from his horse and broken three ribs but was protesting that he was well and fit for work; this had apparently not been mentioned in his letter to her. She also learnt that some of her letters had arrived in England and were being laid before the Court of Directors of the East India Company. On 20 May Lady Macnaghten and some of the ladies breakfasted with Dost

Mohammed Khan and his *harem*: a breach of protocol as no men were supposed to be present when their womenfolk entertained guests. The agenda was made plain by a servant from Kandahar who spoke Hindi and told the European ladies not to believe a word Dost Mohammed said about the power struggle in Kabul or the hostages as he was deliberately misleading them.

The 21 May was a good day for Lady Sale for she received two short letters from her husband dated 15 May. He had been congratulated by Lord Ellenborough and Sir Jasper Nicholls (commander-in-chief of HM forces in India) for holding Jalalabad and defeating Akbar Khan. The 35th Bengal Regiment Native Infantry was to be honoured by being made light infantry, the Company's troops would be given medals bearing the word 'J' and a mural crown on their colours. Ellenborough was to ask Queen Victoria that Sale's European Regiment, the 13th of Foot, should be given similar honours. More practically, the ladies were sent cloth, sugar candy, tea and cheese from Jalalabad, whilst the gentlemen received boots and shoes. Lady Sale, in high good humour, repeated a joke Akbar Khan made when his followers asked him about which tent he would like to have when he left Tezeen for Kabul: 'The ladies and people above have got all our tents here; but you may send my *salaam* to General Sale and ask him to lend me one of those he took from me' (*Journal*, 351).

The mood became more sombre the following day when the prisoners heard that ponies had arrived to take them to Kabul. The officers went to Dost Mohamed Khan and protested that only thirty-three ponies and no camels were available and that these were inadequate for the transport of such a large party, so the order to depart was delayed until the following day. But Akbar and his followers were determined to keep their prisoners close in the face of an expected British attack. Mules arrived on 23 May but only enough to carry three panniers; there were no camels but the planned road was, in any case, unsuitable for them. The prisoners travelled for 22 miles through the Huft Kotul pass. Initially Lady Sale waxed lyrical about the warmer weather and the flowers: 'The yellow briar-rose is in bloom, and asphodels of three different colours, yellow, pink and greenish brown, a pretty description of borage, and a plant resembling sage with a red flower' (*Journal*, 352). The pass, however, was to become 'both to the sight and smell equally offensive' as many bodies from the January retreat still lay there and Lady Sale was particularly distressed that she could still recognise the corpse of 'poor Major Ewart'. They reached the fort at Khoord Kabul at 6.00 pm; it was the same one that they had occupied in January.

The following day they travelled for about 19 miles, making difficult ascents and descents of the hills. Lady Sale's pony, for which she had paid 2 rupees 6 anas made heavy weather of these obstacles but she preferred riding to walking. They passed the famous 'pillar of Alexander', which was in poor condition; the workmanship clearly predated the Afghan period and Eyre, the artist, gave a more precise description of its classical features (Eyre, *Military Operations at Cabul*, 317). Locals tended to attribute any ancient monument of unknown origin to Alexander, or 'Sikunder' as he was called. It had been intended that they should go to Mohammed Shah Khan's fort but he wished to keep it for his family. They were now only 3 miles from Kabul but were offered inferior accommodation: two open stables or cowsheds down a narrow valley at Meer Akor's fort at Noor Mohammed (Shewaki). Incensed, Lady Sale went with Lieutenant Melville to Dost Mohamed Khan to protest.

Some of the prisoners were then given a small room over the gateway of the inner fort and were promised better quarters the following day. Lady Sale spent a miserable night, still troubled by the wound in her wrist, and hearing firing from Kabul that they were told was an assault by Akbar Khan on the Bala Hissar. Once the Afghan ladies were removed from the fort on 25 May the prisoners were given better accommodation, as had been promised:

> In addition to the two rooms apportioned to our party, we have permission to sit, in the daytime, in a room in a *bourj* (tower), a small octagon with *oorsees* or open-work lattices. There are two flights of steep steps to mount it from our apartments, which are upstairs; but the view from it is so refreshing, looking over all the forts and highly cultivated grounds; it has the advantage of being always cool; and which compensates for the trouble of getting there.
>
> (*Journal*, 356)

Their gaoler, Ali Mohammed Khan a Kuzzilbashi, seems to have treated them well and this fort was to be their home for more than three months.

CHAPTER 6

'I Think He Will Not Cut Our Throats', Bamian and Freedom

The last months of the prisoners' captivity were particularly trying. Many were afflicted by diseases brought on by the warmer weather, and Akbar Khan, involved in resistance to the British campaign that finally started in the summer, no longer protected them. He sent them to Bamian where they might easily have been murdered but instead they managed to secure their freedom by bribery, since as British power increased again some Afghans were prepared to deal with them. The Indian government was glad to hail the occupation of Kabul and the release of the prisoners as a great victory.

During the last days of May the prisoners in the fort at Shewaki believed, wrongly, that General Pollock had marched as far as Gandamack: in fact he was still to wait for over two months at Jalalabad whilst Ellenborough made up his mind what to do. More accurate was the news that Akbar Khan was trying to inveigle Shah Shujah's son, Futteh Jung, into leaving the Bala Hissar but, fearing that he would meet the same fate as his father, he was staying put as he still received some assistance, especially from the Kuzzilbashis. Shah Zeman Khan was only lukewarm in his support of the *Sirdar* and the merchants of Kabul wanted the British to return because fewer rupees had been circulating since their departure.

The prisoners heard that Pollock had offered to exchange them for Akbar's four wives and their children in India but it was unlikely that he would settle for anything less than the return of his whole family, including the Dost his father. In the face of a constantly expected British advance Akbar had every reason to keep the prisoners with him whilst he decided on his next move and that was unlikely to be made until the British generals showed their hand. Nott at Kandahar and Sale at Jalalabad might eventually retreat to India or they might attack Ghazni and Kabul. Akbar was desperately short of money and he hoped to exact a ransom from the British as well as guarantees of his personal safety, hopes that were illusory.

The prisoners were kept under an ever closer guard, previously the officers had been allowed to go out of the fort to bathe but this was now forbidden. The ladies could walk in the garden but all were locked into the central part at night and servants could not leave for any purpose without a guard. Captain Troup, however, was trusted by the *Sirdar* to act as a go-between for him, the prisoners and General Sale: the political agents Lawrence and Mackenzie already had some freedom of action. On 4 June Troup brought two parcels from Jalalabad, one for Lady Sale and one for distribution amongst the ladies. Lady Sale was also delighted by her husband's letter which included copies of the congratulations he had received from Lord Ellenborough and Sir Jasper Nicholls. She shook off her fever and, 'in the gladness of my heart felt quite well again'. Ellenborough had already honoured Sale and his army with the title 'the illustrious garrison'. Akbar gave the prisoners cloth, soap, candles and a washbasin (*chillumchee*), the latter perhaps a sign that he expected them to stay at the fort for some time.

Lady Sale, despite all the disinformation she received, gave an astute assessment of the balance of power in Kabul at this time:

> Though Akbar is superior in rank, Mahommed Shah has the troops, and what money they can raise at command. Sultan Jan is the fighting arm of the trio, under the latter; whilst Akbar sits in *durbar* [meetings], laughs, talks and squeezes all who are suspected of having money. He has carefully kept all our notes to him, asking for or thanking him for things received: no doubt to produce at the last; as a further proof of his kindness to his captives.
>
> (*Journal*, 361–2)

She also commented on the speed with which the Afghans could assemble fighting men in contrast to the musters of British troops. She attributed this to the fact that from childhood all males owned at least one knife and

69

required only a pistol, a *jezail* and, perhaps, a horse to become an effective soldier. *Jezails* were superior to British muskets as they had a longer range and Akbar's heavy guns were being serviced by men who had deserted from the British army earlier in the year. There was also the religious factor, *mullahs* and *ghazis* threatened eternal damnation to those who would not fight and promised paradise filled with *houris* (beautiful maidens) to those who were killed in a religious war.

Captain Mackenzie came from the *Sirdar* on 9 June bringing newspapers and letters from Jalalabad that had been intercepted by Akbar. He assured the prisoners that Futteh Jung had surrendered the Bala Hissar and was now in Akbar's power. During the siege that preceded Futteh's capitulation, Akbar's father-in-law and Sultan Jan had both been wounded when an explosion sent stones falling on their heads. Pollock's force was still in Jalalabad suffering from sickness caused by the great heat. The prisoners' guard had been increased by thirty men and it remained difficult to get reliable news from anyone other than the officers who were allowed to carry messages. Akbar must have realised that now they were near Kabul with its Hindu merchants and Afghans who were pro-British it was harder to control his captives. A respectable young man who brought goods for Captain Johnson was arrested, fined 6,000 rupees and had all his nails torn out. A Hindu was stopped at the gate and severely beaten because he was suspected of bringing in news and another was beaten and had his horse confiscated.

There were, however, lighter moments. Lady Sale paid 1 rupee and whilst they were in the fort's garden she and her daughter were given: the finest mulberries the garden produced . . . nicely cooled by the rill of the stream, and covered with a shower of roses. We filled our basket; and sat and ate the fruit under the vines; and look forward to delicious sherbet from the flowers tomorrow' (*Journal*, 370). Their living conditions had also become more tolerable: Lady Sale and her daughter now shared a room with Lady Macnaghten, Mrs Mainwaring, Mrs Boyd and their children. The little Mainwaring boy was a favourite and was known as 'Jung-i-Bahadur' ('Mighty in Battle'). Captain Boyd gallantly slept on either the landing or the roof: 'After so long enduring the misery of having gentleman night and day associated with us, we found this a great relief' (*Journal*, 404).

The following days were plagued by rumours about what the British armies were doing, who was most powerful in Kabul and the probable fate of the prisoners. Gunfire was heard from time to time and all that was certain was that Akbar was quarrelling with the other leaders and that the prisoners needed his protection against the *ghazis* who would have been happy to butcher them. On 25 June Lady Sale received fairly accurate news, presumably from Captains Mackenzie and Troup who joined them on that day. Nott was still in Kandahar but Kalat-i-Ghilzai had been abandoned and destroyed. The scandalous Mrs Wade continued her nefarious activities (Lady Sale had tried without success to get little Stoker transferred from her custody to the care of Mrs 'Burnes' and he later died). The soldiers who had remained at Buddeabad had suffered terribly from the heat and were attacked by fever: their only remedy was bleeding with a penknife wielded by Mr Blewitt, the clerk, in which he was 'very successful'. Sergeant Reynolds, who had a broken arm, had died of lockjaw. The surviving troops from Buddeabad actually joined the prisoners the following day 'miserably thin and weak' (Eyre, *Military Operations at Cabul*, 329). They also heard about the sufferings of Colonel Charles Stoddart and Captain Arthur Conolly, the political agents who had been imprisoned by the ferocious ruler of Bokara. In fact they had both been beheaded there during June: a terrible example of what could happen to captive Europeans.

The heat in early July started to affect the prisoners: Mackenzie, Lawrence, Waller and Melville all had fever and 'Mrs Burnes's' child died, probably of the same cause. By 11 July two more prisoners and several Hindu servants had also caught it. They were still troubled from time to time by earthquakes, although none proved to be as violent as that of 19 February. Mrs Trevor, whose husband had been murdered in Kabul, gave birth to a baby girl. Captain Troup, who replaced the sick Mackenzie as a go-between, had left for Jalalabad taking letters and part of Lady Sale's *Journal* with him, the visit forming part of the continuing negotiations over the fate of the prisoners. Akbar cannot have been aware that Pottinger had sent a letter with Troup to General Pollock that showed his judicious sensitivity to Indian opinion:

At present I do not think it would be advisable to ransom us for money, as he [Akbar] is in want of that necessary; and the name and character of the British must suffer in the opinion of our own subjects and soldiers in India, if we were to pay for the release of a few Europeans, while so many thousands of our native soldiery and camp-followers are reduced to slavery throughout this country, and many other poor, wretches, deprived of their hands and feet or otherwise mutilated or diseased, are supporting their precarious existence by beggary. If these latter persons be not released, many, if not all, must perish in the ensuing winter; and it appears to me that Government will lay itself open to the odium of undue partiality if it release us by ransom.

(Mackenzie, vol. 1, 353–4)

These remnants of the soldiery and the camp followers had escaped death so far, partly by conversion to Islam (as Mackenzie states elsewhere) and slavery, and partly by the charitable support of Hindu merchants and other well-disposed inhabitants of Afghanistan.

Meanwhile, Captain Mackenzie's health, he was suffering from typhus, was causing such anxiety that Dr Campbell, one of the doctors who had been left behind in Kabul with the wounded in January, came to the fort to attend him. He was eventually nursed back to health by the devoted care of the Eyres and the Rileys. On 18 July the prisoners were visited by Akbar Khan (now called *Wuzeer* (vizier) to Futteh Jung, who remained the puppet king), Sultan Jan and Mohammed Shah Khan who sat in the garden and ate all the fruit, much to Lady Sale's disgust. The prisoners did, however, receive letters and newspapers that Akbar had kept back for over a month. Some of her jewellery was restored to Lady Macnaghten in a very broken condition, 'they *talk* of giving back the rest'. This visit by the three most powerful Afghan leaders in Kabul was probably a sign of their increasing anxiety about the approach of the British armies, especially as some of the prisoners, their insurance policy, were sick and dying.

Alexandrina Sturt gave birth to a girl on 24 July: fortunately for mother and child, despite rumours, the prisoners were to remain in the fort for some time to come. Captain Troup returned from Jalalabad three days later with the accurate news that no progress had been made over the exchange of prisoners. Major Pottinger, the senior political agent, had been sidelined by Akbar Khan and Lady Sale remarked that General Pollock also shunned him and the other political agents (probably on instructions from Ellenborough who disliked the breed), so Troup remained the go-between. 'Troup, who purchased a quantity of things of all kinds for us at Jellalabad, *opened up his shop*; and I procured arrow root, cotton gloves, reels of cotton, tape, soap, jalap [a purgative drug], and cream of tartar . . . He expects to be sent to Jelallabad, and I gave him more of my *Journal*, to take to Sale' (*Journal*, 387).

Troup brought Captain Lawrence the welcome news that his brother Henry, who was at Jalalabad commanding a contingent of Sikhs, was 'looking well and hearty'. Lady Sale now knew the British plan of campaign but she was understandably sceptical about it:

Nott is to go to Ghuznee to receive the prisoners [the soldiers taken there]: not to fight, but only to defend himself if attacked; and then come here and join Pollock: and, having received us, all are to walk back hand in hand. We are not to attack Cabul etc., but to evacuate the country; with Akbar, the Ghilzyes, the Barukzyes [family of Dost Mohammed], and all the other Zyes hanging on our flanks and rear: and if they can but get us to procrastinate, so as to give them the advantage of their faithful ally the snow, the Affghans will have the satisfaction of destroying another and still larger army this year.

(*Journal*, 388)

Akbar Khan had not been at all satisfied with Pollock's response to his overtures and so Troup was sent back to Jalalabad, this time accompanied by Lawrence. Lady Sale and Dr Campbell were anxious that he should make such a dangerous and arduous journey since he was still recovering from fever and Akbar wished to keep him at Shewaki as he was: 'the only person who could manage the ladies and children' (Lawrence, 203). Despite their fears he went; on their way they encountered Corporal Lewis of the 44th who was being held prisoner by a chieftain. To save his life he had pretended to convert to Islam and he begged the officers to take him with them. The chief was disgusted to find that his conversion was

73

insincere but, possibly because the two personable officers were his guests, allowed the three of them to go on to Jalalabad where Lawrence was joyfully but briefly re-united with his brother Henry. The guide was surprised that when they met they only shook hands rather than embracing, 'you are an extraordinary people, I cannot make you out'.

Pollock was annoyed at the haughty tone of Akbar's message and felt that this excused him from honouring a verbal agreement that he had formerly made to make substantial concessions in return for the release of the prisoners. This was not a pleasant message for Lawrence and Troup to be obliged to take back to the *Sirdar*. He had planned to receive a substantial ransom and a promise that he would be pardoned in exchange for the prisoners but the British had decided to advance on Kabul ending his hopes. His periodic threats to send the prisoners off to be sold as slaves reflect his frustration.

At the end of the month the prisoners were disturbed to hear that three ponies sent to them from Jalalabad had been stolen. It was annoying to lose the money and letters that they carried but, most serious, was the loss of medicines as most of the party was suffering from fever. Rice was cultivated in the valley and the stagnant water bred mosquitoes that tormented them and had probably spread malaria: the hostage Lieutenant Conolly who was visiting the prisoners (the brother of the man who had been murdered at Bokara) was to die a week later. Eyre lamented his fate believing that, but for his efforts, the sick and wounded in Kabul would have died either of starvation or at the hands of fanatics. The other five officer hostages in Kabul joined the prisoners at this time. Lice were another source of discomfort, these they called 'infantry' and the famous Afghan fleas they called 'light cavalry'. The servants had few clothes so tended to be the worst infected, vermin were passed to the children they cared for and thus to the adults. This could be why several of the officers, who were wearing Afghan clothing, had shaved their heads (Illustration 8). But the climate continued to take its toll and Mrs Smith, the servant of Mrs Trevor, died of fever.

The group heard some accurate news on 15 August: that Nott had at last left Kandahar and would advance on Kabul via Moquor and Ghazni (see

Part II, Chapter 4). Akbar Khan said that he had sent 5,000 men to oppose them, and if the Jalalabad force moved up the prisoners could be sent at half an hour's notice to a fine climate with plenty of ice: they correctly surmised that would be Bamian. Lady Sale comforted herself with the thought that, although the situation was precarious, Akbar: 'will not cut our throats; - not out of love to us, but because the other chiefs would resent it; as, having possession of us, they could at least obtain a handsome sum as our ransom' (*Journal*, 389). Futteh Jung had escaped from Kabul and made his way to Pollock's army (when he arrived there he was in a weak and ragged state). Akbar Khan's schemes were slowly unravelling but this was not, as yet, apparent to the prisoners.

The opinions in the British and Indian newspapers sent from Jalalabad both annoyed and amused Lady Sale. One castigated her for being too partial to Akbar Khan while another objected that she only wrote as she did because she was a prisoner: an equally aggravating sentiment to one who never minced her words. This led her to make a summary of what had occurred since the beginning of the year. On the one hand, she condemned the cruelty and duplicity of the *Sirdar* and his fellow leaders and expressed the wish that they should be defeated to prove the superiority of British civilised values. On the other hand, she felt that the prisoners had been treated as decently as was practical since mid-January, although the sufferings of their servants were worse:

> As to the justice of dethroning the Ameer Dost Mahommed, and setting up Shah Shujah, I have nothing to say regarding it: nor regarding our policy in attempting to keep possession of a country of uncivilised people, so far from our own; whence all supplies of ammunition, money etc. must be obtained. Let our Governors-General and Commanders-in-Chief look to that; whilst I knit socks for my grand-children: but I have been a soldier's wife too long to sit down tamely, whilst our honour is tarnished in the sight and opinion of savages.
>
> (*Journal*, 401)

She was, however, amused by the reports of some papers, 'regarding my wonderful self' in which she was alleged to have led the troops on the retreat. The only thing that gave her pleasure was the news that civilians in India were making a subscription to purchase a sword to present to her husband, who would value it most highly. In retrospect the prisoners, hostages and sick and wounded were well treated by the Afghans compared to the fate suffered by prisoners during the Indian Mutiny. In Bengal, fifteen years later, hundreds of European soldiers, civilians, women, children and Indian Christians were deliberately murdered by mutinous regiments of the army.

Lady Sale astutely observed that, despite brave words from Akbar Khan, he was unlikely to do battle in the open field with the British armies when they arrived in Kabul. The impenetrable parts of his country away from that city would enable him to resist attack successfully 'with any rabble he can collect'. The surviving prisoners from Ghazni joined the larger party on 23 August: Colonel Palmer, four captains and four lieutenants including Lieutenant Harris (see Part II, Chapter 4). Shumshoodeen Khan feared that his stronghold was about to be attacked by Nott and wished to put these assets beyond reach and Sultan Jan was said to be taking 300 men from Kabul to reinforce him.

The long-expected order to leave the vicinity of Kabul came on 25 August, although a number of the sick had to be left behind in the fort. These included Captain and Mrs Anderson and Mrs Trevor with their children with Dr Campbell to care for them (they never rejoined the main body of prisoners and were liberated separately): a soldier had died of fever that day. The rest of the party left in the evening, seen off by the indefatigable Captain Troup (who remained with Akbar, as did Captain Bygrave), riding 50 ponies and guarded by about 300 Afghans. The women and children, apart from Lady Sale, rode in camel panniers, as did ten soldiers who were ill with fever; Captain Mackenzie was still sick, as was Lieutenant Eyre. He recorded that most of the ladies had adopted the *burka* to give them more protection in the wild and unknown regions to which they were being taken. Lady Sale did not mention this: she probably thought that it was demeaning and retained her European dress as more practical for riding.

The party made a detour to avoid Kabul, crossed the Loghur river, and stopped after about 18 miles at a fort at Killa Kazee. They were to sleep during the heat of the day and travel the following night but they had to find what shade they could outside the fort as it was occupied by Sultan Jan and his reinforcements for Ghazni. During the morning Dr Berwick, Lieutenants Evans and Haughton and the thirty-four European soldiers who had been sick or wounded joined the prisoners. Lieutenant Conolly had helped them but they probably owed their survival to Zeman Shah Khan who was moderate and compassionate in his dealings with the British and who had sheltered them. There were insufficient animals to transport everyone so some of these soldiers and Lieutenant Haughton, who was still recovering from the horrors of a second amputation, were left behind.

Relationships between the prisoners and their keepers seem to have soured at this time for the Europeans hated the prospect of leaving Kabul just as their armies were advancing. The Afghans, freed from the unpredictable but generally chivalrous surveillance of Akbar Khan, became surly and hostile. When Sultan Jan (Sir William Macnaghten's grey was spotted amongst his fine horses) left the fort in the course of the day some of the officers went to prepare a room for the women and children, as had been promised. This was refused and they were asked rudely how as *kaffirs* they dared wear their shoes there. Lady Sale and Lieutenant Eyre took their revenge in their writing by making fun of the awful noise the Afghans made on the 'musical' instruments they had stolen from the British army. She also commented on the naïvety of the sentries who stood guard with muskets, also taken from the British, holding the ramrods as weapons and leaving the guns stuck in the earth.

The prisoners left their camp after midnight on 27 August and ascended the Bala Maidan through an attractive valley: 'thickly studded with forts and diversified with cultivation; with lines of willows and poplars marking the water cuts; which here serve as hedgerows' (*Journal*, 415). They stopped at a fort but were accommodated in five tents. Some of the officers started to plan their escape by attempting to bribe the chieftain who was in charge of them, they hoped to persuade him to make short marches away from Kabul and eventually to hand them over to General Nott. Lady Sale had not been consulted about this plan and was annoyed that she and her daughter would have been expected to contribute 5,000 rupees each (that they did not have). She could also have been irritated that Lady Macnaghten had been valued at 10,000 rupees! This first attempt to secure their freedom came to nothing.

The following day they left the camp at 2.00 pm and travelled to Tarkana, which they reached in the evening. Had Lady Sale: 'taken the ride for my own amusement on a good horse, instead of being driven about as a captive on a sorry baggage *yaboo* (pony), I should have enjoyed it very much' (*Journal*, 416). She gave an enthusiastic description of the beautiful scenery and when they stopped and camped on green grass they were sheltered from the sun by a double row of poplars. They acquired small fish and some poor quality fruit that had just arrived by caravan but the commander of the guard spoilt the idyllic mood by stealing five of their camels. As the prisoners ascended to higher ground the weather cooled, they could see snow in some places, so the need to travel at night ended.

They marched 8 more miles on 29 August and lost two more camels to their guards. The following day they progressed 16 miles to Gurdundar on the Helmand river meeting a man who claimed to be a messenger from Ghazni who gave them the encouraging (but inaccurate) news that it had fallen to the British and that they were about to be released. Their guards later attacked a small party of Hazaras killing one and taking some loot and two captives; they were bitter enemies of the Pashtu Afghans and lived in separate villages (see Part II, Chapter 4). The next day they travelled to the Hadje Gurk pass where Lady Sale was impressed by the massive stone figures which she imagined were ancient Buddhist or Brahmin remains. There were worrying signs in the dilapidated condition of a fort and the sound of gunfire that conflict with the Hazaras was taking place in the area. The next morning they ascended the pass without incident, crossed the river and camped by a fort.

Between 1 and 3 September the journey continued to Bamian through harsh country, although the valleys were cultivated with corn and beans. On their arrival the prisoners refused accommodation in a wretched fort and preferred to stay in their tents despite the fact that their captors found them easier to guard in forts. Their camp was near the largest of the two great images of Buddha that dominated the area: the guards cursed them as idols and shot at them. The local war-lord who now had charge of them was Saleh Mohammed Khan; Low said that he had formerly been a member of Hopkins's Afghan Regiment (Low, 339). His wife, who was young, fat and fair and was reputed to have been a dancing girl in Ludianah, visited Lady Macnaghten. During the following five days: 'we made excursions to see the caves, etc. At first some difficulty was made: but the General sent some thirty men to guard us and our pencils; for several went intent on sketching. I only copied the frescoes that were on the walls and ceiling near the large image; but Mr Eyre made some very pretty and correct sketches of Ghoolghoola (the ancient city)' (*Journal*, 422–3). Lady Sale was longing to visit the city but was refused on the grounds that the guards had enough to do.

To make the problem of guarding the increased number of prisoners less onerous they were transferred on 9 September to 'one of these horrid forts'. Although it had previously been occupied by Dr Lord (formerly a political agent at Bamian who had been killed in action against Dost Mohammed in November 1840), the only accommodation they were given was a number of vermin-infested sheds. Lady Sale, her daughter and the *ayah*, assisted by Mr Melville who was sleeping elsewhere, set to and made their cowshed as habitable as possible, forming a rough window. Captain Lawrence reported that he and the other officers slept in a courtyard where he was greatly annoyed by a huge jackass that brayed all night. He let it loose several times hoping that it would be quiet but eventually the guards threatened to brain him if he did so again. The situation was, however, about to improve dramatically.

The prisoners had been advised by a sepoy, who had deserted from the British army, that there were about fifty Hindus in their guard (also deserters) who would be willing to join them and that 'Saleh Mahommed Khan was a man who would do anything for money'. When Captains Johnson and Lawrence first sounded out the chieftain on the subject he treated it as a joke but, on 11 September, he showed that he had taken the offer of a large bribe seriously. Lady Sale allowed the two officers plus Captains Mackenzie and Webb and Major Pottinger (whose command of Persian was a great asset) to use her room as the most private place in the fort. Sitting on the bed they made a solemn agreement to give Saleh Mohammed 20,000 rupees as a lump sum and 1,000 rupees a month for life. If the British government did not pay him the money, the prisoners would guarantee it out of their own resources and they signed a paper, heading it in the name of Jesus Christ, to prove their sincerity. Like many Afghans, Saleh Mohammed seemed to feel no particular loyalty to Akbar Khan: the following day he hoisted the standard of defiance on the walls, white with a crimson edge and a green fringe.

The Europeans and their servants could no longer be described as prisoners and Eldred Pottinger (sidelined when Akbar Khan was around) smoothly resumed his former role as senior political agent. In fact, he acted almost like an Afghan provincial governor, accepting the allegiance of two Hazara chieftains and several Afghan leaders. One conveniently gave Saleh Mohammed 1,000 rupees and this was used to buy dresses of honour from a passing caravan to give to those who came in. The officers set about acquiring muskets and bought some corn so they could hold out if they were besieged. The only dissenters were Brigadier Shelton and Colonel Palmer (Lady Sale excused the latter on the grounds of his sufferings at Ghazni: he was probably experiencing post-traumatic stress) but both eventually agreed to the new situation. Lady Sale wrote to her husband: 'informing him of our resolution to hold out until we received assistance, even should we be reduced to eating the rats and mice; of which we have a grand stock' (*Journal*, 428). Besides their dresses of honour, Pottinger supplied the chiefs with any official documents, empowering them to receive government rents etc. that they requested. They were worthless, although he executed them with an air 'of great condescension and with the gravity of a judge'.

A letter arrived from Mohan Lal confirming reports that Kabul had risen against Akbar Khan and his supporters; Zeman Khan had fled and the Kuzzilbashis had declared in favour of the British. A light force had been sent from the conquering army to rescue the Europeans who they still believed to be imprisoned, so encouraged by this information the party started on their return journey to Kabul on 16 September. They were apprehensive that they might be attacked by forces loyal to Akbar but, when

1. Shah Shujah at the Bala Hissar, 1842, J. Atkinson, *Sketches in Afghaunistan*. The Shah appears on the balcony. (New York Public Library, Digital Gallery)

2. Major 'Fighting Bob' Sale rescues a soldier from attack by a Burmese chief, near Rangoon, 8 July 1824. (Military Museum Taunton)

3. Lady Florentia Sale, lithograph from a watercolour by V. Eyre, *Cabul Prisoners* (London, 1843).

4. The main street in the bazaar in Kabul during the fruit season, 1842, J. Atkinson, *Sketches in Afghaunistan*. (New York Public Library, Digital Gallery)

5. Akbar Khan, V. Eyre, *Cabul Prisoners* (London, 1843). (National Army Museum)

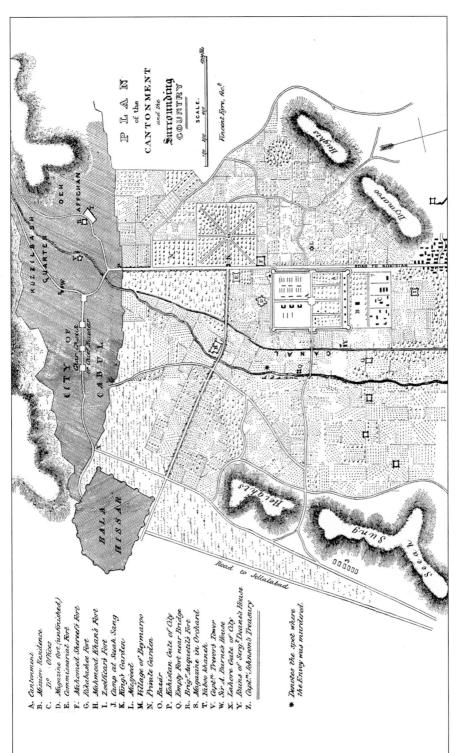

A. Cantonment.
B. Mission Residence.
C. D.° Offices.
D. Magazine fort (unfinished).
E. Commissariat Fort.
F. Mahomed Shereef's Fort.
G. Rikabashee Fort.
H. Mahmood Khan's Fort.
I. Zoolficar Fort.
J. Camp at Seeah Sang.
K. King's Garden.
L. Musjeed.
M. Village of Bejmaroo.
N. Private Garden.
O. Bazar.
P. Kohistan Gate of City.
Q. Empty Fort near Bridge.
R. Brig.ʳ Anquetil's Fort.
S. Magazine in Orchard.
T. Kaboo khaneh.
V. Capt.ⁿ Trevor's Tower.
W. Sir A. Barnes House.
X. Lahore Gate of City.
Y. Ruins of Serg.ᵗ Deane's House.
Z. Capt.ⁿ Johnson's Treasury.

* Denotes the spot where
  the Envoy was murdered.

6. The cantonments in Kabul, 1841, V. Eyre, *The Military Operations at Cabul* . . . (London, 1843).

7. Lieutenant Vincent Eyre, self-portrait, *Cabul Prisoners* (London, 1843). (National Army Museum)

8. A prison scene, V. Eyre, *Cabul Prisoners* (London, 1843). (National Army Museum)

9. Captain Colin Mackenzie when a prisoner wearing Afghan dress, V. Eyre, *Cabul Prisoners* (London, 1843). (National Army Museum)

10. Daniel Wilson, Bishop of Calcutta and Metropolitan of India, 1832–58, Phillips RA 1832, engraved by W. Holl.

11. The Mugger Tullao (crocodile tank) at Karachi, lithograph by T. Picken from a drawing by the Reverend I. Allen, 1843, photograph Peter Fawcett.

12. Afghan fighters in their winter dress with *jezails,* James Rattray, *Costumes of the Various Tribes . . . of Afghaunistan from Original Drawings* (London, 1848).

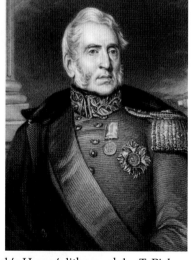

13. General Sir William Nott GCB, by T. Brigstocke, 1844, photograph Peter Fawcett.

14. Kandahar, to the right is the hill called 'The Bullock's Hump', lithograph by T. Picken from a drawing by the Reverend I. Allen, 1843, photograph Peter Fawcett.

15. Ghazni, lithograph by T. Picken from a drawing by the Reverend I. Allen, 1843, photograph Peter Fawcett.

16. The Bala Hissar and Kabul from the upper part of the citadel, 1842, J. Atkinson, *Sketches in Afghaunistan.* (New York Public Library, Digital Gallery)

17. Mosque at the tomb of the Emperor Babur near Kabul, lithograph by T. Picken from a drawing by the Reverend I. Allen, 1843, photograph Peter Fawcett.

18. Ali Musjid in the Khyber pass, lithograph by T. Picken from a drawing by the Reverend I. Allen, 1843, photograph Peter Fawcett.

19. Sir Robert Sale by George Clint, 1843. (Military Museum Taunton)

20. Lady Florentia Sale by George Clint, 1843. (Military Museum Taunton)

Saleh Mohammed Khan rode up and offered them some muskets, none of the soldiers would take them. Outraged, Lady Sale offered to take one herself and lead the party, but even this did not shame anyone into volunteering. She did, however, concede in her 'Addenda' at the end of the *Journal* that the following day half a dozen artillery men requested and obtained muskets. They camped at Killa Topchee near some forts and received a letter bearing the good news that Pollock had forced the Khoord Kabul pass in the face of stiff resistance. They were also informed (inaccurately) that Nott had attacked and pursued the Afghans as far as Siah Sung in Kabul and that Akbar, his cousin, and father-in-law had disappeared. This confirmed Lady Sale's forecast that Akbar and his friends would simply 'take to the hills' until the British left.

The group travelled 11 miles to the foot of the Kaloo pass on 17 September and, at 3.00 pm after their arrival, were sheltering from the sun under the walls of one of the forts when Sir Richmond Shakespear rode up with his 600 Kuzzilbashi horse. He was General Pollock's military secretary and had a reputation as a dashing soldier. Lady Sale's dislike of Brigadier Shelton is clear from her account: she seldom mentioned him except when he was 'croaking' or being unpleasant. On this momentous occasion he was true to form, taking Sir Richmond to task for failing to salute him first as the senior military man, although to do so would have obliged him to ignore the ladies and officers who acclaimed him as he rode past. They were now, at last, given accurate information about the British armies: Nott had gained two victories at Ghazni and Maidan and Pollock had beaten Akbar at Jugdulluk and Tezeen. Sale had been hit by a spent ball but without injury and, to his wife's delight, had been awarded the highest order of the Bath by Queen Victoria, a distinction unprecedented for one of his rank.

The following day they marched to Gundundewar over a stony road and again crossed the Hadje Gurk pass and camped on the banks of the river Helmand. Shakespear was uneasy about the safety of his charges, as Sultan Jan was thought to be in the vicinity, and had written to Pollock to send a brigade to meet him. Nott was quite close and was asked to go but refused, much to his officers' disgust, on the grounds that his men had just arrived

81

and were tired after their long journey. Some writers believe that he was sulking because Pollock, rather than he, had been appointed commander-in-chief of the 'army of retribution'. On 19 September, his sixtieth birthday, General Sale set off with a brigade at a few hours' notice. He left his infantry to guard the pass at Kote Ashruffee and rode at the head of the 3rd dragoons to meet his family and the rest of the party.

Lady Sale believed that the group would have been recaptured had it not been for his arrival, which scared off potential attackers. Of 20 September she wrote:

> It is impossible to express our feelings on Sale's approach. To my daughter and myself happiness so long delayed, as to be almost unexpected, was actually painful, and accompanied by a choking sensation, which could not obtain the relief of tears. When we arrived where the infantry were posted, they cheered all the captives as they passed them; and the men of the 13th [Sale's regiment] pressed forward to welcome us individually. Most of the men had a little word of hearty congratulation to offer, each in his own style, on the restoration of his colonel's wife and daughter: and then my highly-wrought feelings found the desired relief; and I could scarcely speak to thank the soldiers for their sympathy, whilst the long with-held tears now found their course. On arriving at the camp, Captain Backhouse fired a royal salute from his mountain train guns.
>
> (*Journal*, 436–7)

The next day, 21 September, they marched to Killa Kazee and had the satisfaction of burning one of Sultan Jan's forts. They were concerned about the whereabouts of Captain Bygrave: he was eventually sent to Pollock by Akbar Khan on 27 September, as a kind of peace offering, the last prisoner to be released. At 3.00 pm they recommenced their journey to Kabul which they soon reached, passing through the Great Bazaar which looked desolate with all the shops shut. When they arrived at Pollock's camp at Siah Sung they were greeted by a salute of twenty-one guns. At that point Lady Sale ended her *Journal*: 'And now my Notes may end. Any further journals of mine can only be interesting to those nearly connected to me' (*Journal*, 438).

Captain Troup, the sick ladies, officers and children who had been left at Shewaki were already at Pollock's camp, conducted there by a friendly chieftain. The total released were, including the hostages taken at Kabul in late December 1841, 20 officers, conductor Riley, 10 ladies, 2 soldiers' wives (presumably including the notorious Mrs Wade, it has been impossible to discover her eventual fate), 22 children, 51 soldiers and 2 clerks. Allen in his *Diary* calculated that 117 prisoners altogether were released, 9 more than the total given here. The scattered locations of the prisoners and questions such as whether clerks and prisoners from Ghazni were to be counted may account for the disparity. Nott does not seem to have taken any of the sepoys who reached Kabul back to India with him. Pollock, on the other hand, took about 2,000 crippled sepoys and camp followers, giving them carriage and food right back to their homes in India. Others, who were not rescued, remained in slavery in Afghanistan including, it was said, a few Europeans (Mackenzie, vol. 1, 369–70).

Some of Lady Sale's letters and parts of her *Journal* were available in India and London during the middle months of 1842 and they were also laid before the Directors of the East India Company. The whole *Journal* was published by John Murray in London in 1843. There can be no doubt that her plucky account of the dangers and discomforts of the retreat from Kabul and the subsequent experiences of the prisoners, and of the sepoys and camp followers who were left to die or to be sold into slavery, rallied British and Indian opinion. The way in which she and the officers refused to be cowed by their captors and made the best of difficult circumstances (for example, cleaning up a cowshed) was inspiring to most of her readers. To her amusement, she and her husband became a popular heroine and hero in the following months and were showered with plaudits and honours. On 15 October, shortly after news of their impending release had reached Britain, the *Illustrated London News* wrote: 'The conduct of all the ladies is spoken of as beyond praise, and such as to make every Englishman prouder still of his countrywomen. Lady Sale and Mrs Sturt continue to afford examples of magnanimity and patient suffering to those of weaker mould' (1842, 356).

PART II

THE REVEREND ISAAC ALLEN'S *DIARY*, APRIL 1841 TO FEBRUARY 1843

CHAPTER 1

The 'Perfect *Griffin*', the Journey Through Sind

The Diary that forms the basis of the second part of this book has a different tone from Lady Sale's Journal. She was a seasoned campaigner but the Reverend Allen was a newcomer to India and probably knew little of the army in which he was to be embedded so we participate in his enthusiasm for the many new sights, sensations and incidents that he experienced. As he was a committed Christian some of his reactions were expressed in religious terms. This first chapter, which covers nearly a year before he joined 'the army of retribution', was something of a honeymoon period before the darker and more dangerous times that were to come.

The Reverend Isaac Nicholson Allen arrived in Bombay by boat from England in April 1841 after a voyage of six months. The fifth son of Samuel Allen, gentleman, of St Catherine's by the Tower, he was thirty-two years old and a graduate of Magdalen Hall, Oxford (a college that no longer exists). He had worked as a curate in England before leaving for India where he had been appointed an Assistant Chaplain in Bombay to the East India Company. There were about 130 such chaplains in India under the overall authority of Bishop Daniel Wilson of Calcutta, the Metropolitan (equivalent to the Archbishop of Canterbury), although Allen's immediate superior was the Bishop of Bombay (Illustration 10). Chaplains had to be under forty, have been in holy orders for at least two years, be in good health and able to pay a bond of £500 as a guarantee that they would perform their duties satisfactorily. In return they were paid the substantial sum of 800 rupees a month, could return to England every seven years and, if they survived for twenty years, receive a full pension.

The East India Company was very sensitive to the negative impact on Indian opinion that would be caused as a result of attempts by its employees to convert Hindus and Muslims to Christianity. Chaplains were strongly discouraged from indulging in such activities and although Allen, from time to time, deplored the superstitious practices of the Indians and Afghans, he never seems to have evangelised them. Instead, he contented himself with praying that in the future they would be enlightened and embrace the true faith.

Allen had no opportunity to take up a peaceful post, as he had no doubt expected, since on 10 May he was ordered by the Bishop of Bombay to travel to Sind to join HM 40th Regiment of Foot, part of the field force under Major-General Richard England. The First Afghan War was then in its third year and the Governor General, Lord Auckland, and his envoy, Sir William Macnaghten, were still deluded that all was well. The army had *cantonments* in Karachi in Lower Sind, whose rulers had been cowed into being co-operative. The camp formed part of a somewhat unsatisfactory line of communications for supplies and reinforcements between the nearest British base in Afghanistan, Kandahar, and 300 miles further on, Kabul. England's force had moved up to Baluchistan but the season was unsuitable for further travel and Allen was not urgently required, so he remained in Karachi until December 1841.

Allen started his *Diary* as soon as he arrived in India but the dramatic episodes that occurred when he joined the force, first in Quetta and then as two brigades assembled at Kandahar and marched to Kabul as part of the 'army of retribution', were described in greater detail. It was published rapidly, in London in 1843, soon after he finished it. The book was dedicated to Lieutenant Colonel Hibbert and the officers and soldiers of HM 40th Foot 'by their faithful friend the Author'. It was illustrated with Allen's drawings of the interesting places he visited on his travels that were turned into lithographs by T. Picken. Allen said that the book was simply a recital of his personal adventures in which he tried clearly to distinguish between what he saw himself and what he was told by others, only touching on wider issues to clarify his narrative. Initially he sent his account in monthly letters to his family but later, when regular communication became impossible, he consolidated it into a book which he believed would be interesting to the public. At the end he added five sermons that he had delivered on some of the most memorable days during the last part of the campaign. He hoped to comfort those who had lost friends and relatives (no bodies were returned to Britain or India and where many lay was unknown) with the news that a church was being built at Colabah, near Bombay, to commemorate them (*Diary*, Preface, vii–viii). This church was founded by the Reverend G. Piggot who knew Allen and who had accompanied the 'army of the Indus' into Afghanistan in 1838/9 and had subsequently returned to India.

'*Griffin*' was the nickname for young men who had newly arrived to take up posts in India. Initially, most found that the very different climate, diet and customs from those that they knew in their native country presented a considerable challenge. Allen was not impressed by Karachi, where he arrived after a miserable voyage on 16 May, it was: 'most unattractive, nor does it greatly improve upon acquaintance . . .the gloomy portal of a desolate and uninteresting country; bleached, barren, and craggy rocks, salt marshes overgrown with mangrove, and deserts of sand as far as the eye can reach, without a particle of verdure, form its characteristics' (*Diary*, 18). Yet he had a cheerful, positive disposition and took his calling as a clergyman very seriously. He soon made friends with a number of officers and their families from the various regiments he found there and was often entertained to meals and accompanied them on excursions. He built himself a bungalow and kept servants, horses and dogs as befitted his status.

Allen usually held two services on Sundays (there were no references to other clergy being present either in Karachi or more forward posts), supervised the school for army children and regularly visited the military hospital. He was distressed to see men consumed by tropical diseases from which they were unlikely to recover and he recounted the history of one in order to draw a moral for his readers. This young man had been a Herefordshire farm worker but had developed dissipated habits and deserted his widowed mother and her younger children to become a soldier. As he lay dying his wickedness weighed heavily on his conscience, although Allen tried to comfort him by praying and assuring him of God's mercy. He also took the opportunity to warn other young men against joining the army precipitately without considering the consequences.

As a '*griffin*' Allen was amused to discover that since officers were living in 'camp fashion', if he was entertained by his friends he had to take his furniture and utensils with him, as every man was only supposed to keep what was sufficient for his own needs. This rule applied when, on 7 July, he accompanied four officers on an excursion to the Mugger Tallao or Crocodile Tank, the shrine of an Islamic saint about 8 miles out of Karachi. This was an attractive place, thickly wooded and approached by two venerated tombs, the fine carving of which Allen compared with work he had seen on Elizabethan and Jacobean buildings in England. Their servants had pitched a large tent for them under a beautiful tamarind tree (Illustration 11). Sheltered from the heat of the sun (about 97 degrees), they spent their time observing the crocodiles that proved to be disappointingly sluggish, even when plagued by pokes and blows from the younger officers. During the night, however, Allen had reason to be thankful that they were so supine as one of his friends aroused him to say that a large one was lurking near their open tent. After remaining awake and apprehensive for some time he finally resumed his sleep until morning.

Allen's pleasant life in Karachi was abruptly terminated on 9 December 1841 when he was instructed by the Bishop of Bombay to go to Kandahar as soon as possible. The 40th had left Quetta some months earlier to march there and General England was urgently required to join them from Baluchistan with a relief brigade. News was arriving of the unrest in Afghanistan and, although the government in India had no conception as yet of the seriousness of the situation, it did realise that more troops had to be sent there. Allen relished adventure and was to prove his coolness in battle: as a bachelor he was an obvious choice to be sent as the only clergyman to accompany the relief force. In 1846 the Reverend G.R. Gleig, Principal Chaplain to the Forces, wrote an account of Sale's brigade in Afghanistan but had remained in Britain throughout the war. It seems that the Reverend Piggot and the Reverend Mr Hammond (who was mentioned by Lieutenant John Samuel Knox, *Nott's Brigade in Afghanistan*, 1) in

1838/9 and Allen in 1842 were the only clergy to venture into Afghanistan during the war.

Captain Thomas of the 8th Bombay Regiment Native Infantry, who was to accompany Allen as far as Shikarpore, left Karachi with him on 14 December. Although Jemedar-ki-Lande, where they stayed the first night, was only fourteen miles away, he found the landscape more attractive than the desolation around the city. Their servants had gone ahead and prepared their breakfast in a bungalow intended for travellers. It was quite common in that climate to rise very early, travel, work or fight and then hope to spend the heat of the day at leisure. On this occasion they dined at 3.00 pm and strolled in the evening to a Muslim graveyard before returning for prayers and a sound sleep. The bungalow had no doors or any kind of guard but they were not alarmed by: 'A hyena . . . munching and cracking bones outside, and the jackals kept up a dismal yelling' (*Diary*, 38).

Allen and Thomas arrived at Tatta, where they were to take a boat up the Indus, on 17 December after enduring several days in which each travellers' bungalow proved to be more sordid and dirty than the last. They had ridden 61 miles and Allen observed that people in England, 'who mount a rail-road carriage' and could travel 200 miles in ten hours, would think this poor progress. In Sind, however, they could go only at the speed of their baggage camels which was 2½ miles an hour. They chose an abandoned *musjid* (mosque) among the old tombs of the kings of Tatta as their camp because it was cleaner and more spacious than the alternatives. They preferred to wait for the boat there, rather than in the squalid town, about 3 miles away.

Whilst they were waiting, Allen carefully examined the imposing tombs that surrounded them, admiring the exquisite carving and the coloured and glazed bricks and drew one of the largest. He also went on a duck-shooting expedition with Thomas, accompanied by nine bearers, to a *tank* (lake) about 5 miles away. They passed an abandoned British military camp where the occupants, a native corps, had been almost destroyed by malaria two years before. They were disappointed once they reached the tank since it was so large that the hundreds of ducks were able to stay in the deep water out of range of their guns. They bagged only one and some snipe but were pleased by the opportunity to see another camp that was reputed to have been made by Alexander the Great.

On Christmas Eve 1841 they were visited by a lieutenant who told them about the rebellion in Kabul and the precarious situation in Afghanistan. Several additional corps had been ordered up from Bombay and some had arrived at Karachi; together with HM 41st Regiment of Foot they were likely to arrive in Tatta very soon. Alarmed at the turn of events, they rode into the town and camped in the travellers' bungalow, a picturesque and decaying building that had formerly been a *factory* (merchant's trading station). Despite the festive season there was little reason to be cheerful in the light of the disturbing news they had received, so Allen contented himself by commending: 'absent friends whom the season called to mind, the affairs of the country, and my own, to the protection of the God of Providence, who cares alike for states and individuals' (*Diary*, 47).

Allen and Thomas rode 6 miles out to the *bunder* (a quay or harbour) on Christmas Day where a detachment of the 40th was waiting for transport, so Allen was able to celebrate the feast with a service, although he had to be brief as the sun was blazing down. He was disappointed by his first sight of the Indus, which was low at that time of year and reminded him of the Thames at Greenwich. During the morning the steamer arrived and the captain entertained Allen and five others to dinner. He enjoyed the conversation and the company but seems to have been feeling rather homesick. On the following day he was gratified when the captain arranged for a service to be held on board with seats and a protective awning, and it was well attended. He said that it was the first service he had heard for two years, which shocked Allen who went on to muse that it was no wonder that, under such circumstances, Christians relapsed into heathenism. He was still sleeping in his tent and, in the evening, held another service there for ten non-commissioned officers and privates. The *bunder* was a favourite resort of jackals whose cries at night were most alarming, 'like the shriek of a human being in intense agony'.

They embarked on 28 December: there were between 400 and 500 native and European soldiers, several officers and the crew distributed between the steamer and a pinnace (a small ship that sometimes accompanied a larger vessel) that was being taken to the Sikh ruler, Ranjit Singh, as a present. Allen seemed to be unaware that he had died in 1839 and that his successors were busily killing each other. Conditions were very cramped: Allen and Thomas shared an extremely small cabin where they were disturbed by the harsh creaking of the iron ship, once it got under way, and the close atmosphere. The shallow state of the river and the rapid formation of sandbanks meant that the boats were constantly running aground which made progress slow and tedious. The British government hoped at this time further to open up Sind by promoting trade on the Indus but the nature of the river made this a challenging enterprise. Allen was, however, pleased by the attractive scenery as they sailed by, which made a welcome contrast to Karachi. On the evening of 29 December the weather was fine, most people went ashore and the native soldiers lit their cooking fires: 'As I walked the deck of the steamer, the effect of these numerous little fires, with the various groups standing or crouching around them, and the moon rising large and broad in the back-ground, and throwing a long ripple over the water, was wild and beautiful in the extreme' (*Diary*, 51–2).

The next day they reached Hyderabad passing the *shikarghurs* or hunting grounds of the *amirs* (rulers). Allen regretted that the finest soil in the country should be denied to the majority 'for the amusement of these despots'. With perhaps unexpected radicalism and vehemence he compared them to the early Norman Kings of England who depopulated areas to gratify their love of the chase. It is possible, of course, that he was voicing a widespread sentiment in British India that contributed in the following year to its annexation of Sind. For some time the British government in India had been attempting to gain more influence there, not only by encouraging the reluctant *amirs* to open up trade via the Indus but recently they had prevailed upon them to accept a permanent resident and a military force in their territory. They were also required to make a substantial payment towards the war in Afghanistan: the *amirs* were not comforted by the assurance that all this was for their own protection since all they wanted was to be left alone.

On 31 December Allen was invited by the two political agents to the British residency for a New Year dinner. He admired the comfortable house, its grounds and especially a compound containing beautiful specimens of deer and antelope. The other guests, besides the captain and officers from the steamer, were two Bengal officers and a lady who delighted the company by playing on a guitar. The evening ended badly, the steamer was collecting wood about a mile up on the other side of the river and the boat that was meant to take them there got hopelessly lost amongst the sandbanks. One of Allen's companions flew into a temper with the coxswain after his cigar had been extinguished by the heavy dew and only flustered the unfortunate man more disastrously. It took five and a half hours to find a way through the sandbanks back to the steamer by which time they were all soaked to the skin. Allen remarked that he would remember New Year 1842 for a long time.

Allen described sights that he viewed from the steamer such as a camp made in 1839 by the 'army of the Indus' now completely covered with water at the foot of the Lakhi mountains and fishermen floating downstream on large earthenware pots into which they popped their catch. He had to make a choice when they stopped at Sehwun for they were taking on wood again and the officers were only given an hour on shore to visit the attractive town. He was anxious to sketch so he stayed behind but later managed to walk some way towards it:

> The bed of the river, left in a great manner dry by the narrowing of the stream, which lay as smooth as a mirror, was covered with native groups, women in gay colours, men in waving drapery of dark blue; and the sound of their chanted songs, modulated to a pleasing tone, floated across the water . . . I have seldom looked on a scene of more tranquil beauty: all its unpleasing features (for a native town is never without them) were concealed by the distance.

> (*Diary*, 60–1)

That night a young recruit of the 40th died of fever. Allen had been worried that he knew little of religion and regretted that many of the European soldiers habitually spoke using 'blasphemous and filthy expletives' for no apparent reason. The lad was buried on the river bank but it was feared that his body would not rest there for long as it would probably be washed away in a few months.

On Sunday 9 January Allen held a service on the deck of the steamer but the noise of the paddle-wheels was so great that it was difficult to make himself heard. On the next day they reached Sukkur, an attractive town surrounded by date and coconut palms where the British army was well established. Allen's friend from Karachi, Captain Stuart of the 8th Bombay Regiment Native Infantry, greeted him and carried him and Captain Thomas off to receive warm hospitality from his family. They found the climate bracing and were delighted to be free of the steamer after two weeks of noise and close confinement.

Allen was to wait at Sukkur for three weeks, 11 January to 2 February 1842, for the arrival of the main body of HM 41st from Karachi, since he was to accompany them through Upper Sind. The detachment of the 40th with whom he had travelled up the Indus remained in the fort at Bukkur on an island in the river, since the Khan of Khairpur had recently given the British permission to keep a garrison there in time of war. Allen was soon to enter more dangerous territory where relaxed strolls and picnics would be out of the question. News was gradually percolating through the passes about the terrible situation faced by the British in Afghanistan and this was to have an unsettling effect on the people and rulers of Sind, at best reluctant hosts to the army.

The Stuarts were Allen's hosts for the first part of his stay in Sukkur, Captain (he was from the same regiment as Stuart) and Mrs Maclean accommodated him for the second part and the time passed very agreeably. He met old friends and acquaintances from Karachi, improved the strength of his boxes for the coming journey and bought four excellent camels. He enjoyed the climate that was hot in the daytime but cold enough to justify a comfortable fire in the evenings. He strolled around the town admiring the attractive residences that the British had made, mostly from old tombs, and the shops kept by Parsee merchants. The *amirs* owned a tigress housed in an insecure wooden cage but she was so fat and well fed that Allen doubted that she would wish to escape. He also commented on the conspicuous affluence of the conductors, who were chosen from the ranks of European NCOs to oversee supplies and ordnance: was there a perception amongst the British that they were lining their pockets? (See

Part I, Chapter 4 for Mackenzie's defence of Mr Riley the conductor and his wife.) He found the dust very troublesome, even worse than in Karachi, an ominous warning of discomforts to come.

Two captains made a large room in their house available to Allen, where he held a service each Sunday morning. The evening service was celebrated for the European soldiers at the fort at Bukkur in a ruinous building with high pointed arches where the ordnance department supplied empty ammunition boxes and planks so that the men could use them as benches. Allen mused on the contrast this presented with the orderly arrangements in English parish churches and on the unimportance of the disputes that arose in them over the position of a pulpit or the ornaments on the communion table: 'surely such external things should not be allowed to cause a breach of Christian charity among members of the same body, the church, and sharers in the same blessed hope, through one common Saviour' (*Diary*, 72–3). He had his first experience of burying a man, a private of the 40th, without a coffin which he found shocking, although he was soon to become accustomed to the practice.

During the three weeks in Sukkur the full extent of the disaster in Afghanistan became known to the British community:

> The news of Burnes' death, which we had heard at Tattah, was followed by that of Sir W.H.M'naughten, and Mr Trevor, and his children, the latter of which turned out a false report. The negotiations with Ackbar Khan, the disastrous retreat upon Jellalabad, the total annihilation of the force, by cold, starvation, and the enemy, with the seizure of the ladies, were announced in rapid succession, keeping us in a fever of anxiety and excitement, not unmingled with apprehensions for the safety of Sukkur, if the Ameers of Sinde should be emboldened to make a sudden attack.
>
> (*Diary*, 73–4)

Allen commented sharply on the 'infatuated and blind' sense of security that had led to the disasters, he feared that since the defences at Sukkur were in a weak state the force was vulnerable to attack from the *amirs*. At the time no one in the army could have known what they would be expected to do: no final decisions were, in fact, to be made for many months. Allen's Metropolitan, Bishop Daniel Wilson of Calcutta, probably expressed the widespread feeling amongst the British in India when he wrote in his *Journal* on 22 January 1842: 'The appalling tidings of the murder of Sir W.H. Macnaghten has filled all Calcutta with fear and astonishment . . . never anything like it had occurred in India! Oh! may God give our country and our rulers hearts to feel, and eyes to see. January 30th . . . We are all disconsolate, for there is reason to believe that treachery may follow our brave fellows as they retire' (Bateman, vol. 2, 194).

Mail was delivered on 27 January and with it news of the birth of the Prince of Wales, which was celebrated by a royal salute from the guns. The main part of the 41st arrived three days later and, by 2 February, they were ready to start their long and dangerous journey to Kandahar. It got off to a bad start when the mess-tent servants, who should have arrived at their first camp in advance to serve breakfast, lost their way. The force had marched 16 miles to Lukkur and the officers were cross and hungry. Even Allen, who had been served breakfast by his hosts before his departure, was put out so, when the mess tent was finally erected in the afternoon, everyone was glad to hear the bugle for dinner.

The next day they rode 10 miles to Shikarpore, where they stayed until 7 February and Allen and Captain Thomas parted company. The army had a semi-permanent camp there as it was a staging post for entering and leaving Afghanistan. Allen reported that it was an important centre for trade, especially in silks, carpets and shields that were manufactured there. Despite his curiosity he dared not go into the town without an escort because of the unrest caused by the news from Kabul. The 8th NI arrived whilst he was there so he was re-united with the Stuarts, his hosts at Sukkur, and other Karachi friends. He was able to hold a service in a large room in the Residency on the Sunday, just before his departure.

The march to Dadur during the next two weeks was relatively uneventful. The only shots that were fired were to discourage thieves: a few camels disappeared but the military cooking pots were saved. Allen now carried two pistols in his belt and was followed by a servant carrying a loaded gun. The weather was trying, veering from dust storms to downpours that, in Allen's eyes, made the camp look like a large cattle fair in England on a rainy day. Yet when they crossed a stretch of desert he was intrigued by the mirages that appeared exotically oriental to him. As they approached the Bolan range it got colder and he was thrilled by his first experience of snow-capped mountains and his Portuguese servant was delighted to touch and taste a piece of ice.

The force arrived at Dadur on Sunday 20 February and Allen was very annoyed for two reasons: General England 'contrary to all regulation' had commandeered the travellers' bungalow for his exclusive use. Until nightfall Allen had to search for a suitable place to pitch his tent losing any opportunity to hold a service or even for 'private devotion and meditation'. He detested Dadur, quoting the Brahuis (a local tribe) saying that: 'no other place of final torment was needed after the formation of Dadur' (*Diary*, 93). The problem was the intense heat that was increased by the town's situation under barren, rocky mountains, an unpleasant contrast to the bracing weather they had recently enjoyed. There was no wind so the atmosphere was 'stagnant' and the presence, no doubt, of large numbers of horses and camels meant that they were plagued by flies.

Theft was such a problem in the camp that Allen gladly accepted an offer from Major Woodhouse, 6th Bombay Regiment Native Infantry, to pitch his tent inside a breastwork occupied by the regiment and he became an honorary member of their mess. He commented on the unfailing kindness and hospitality he had encountered in India and provided an explanation: 'every man's rank and position is clearly determined; his character, too, in a short time is pretty generally known, and he and all by whom he is entertained, are in one and the same service, whether in the ecclesiastical, civil, or military branch of it' (*Diary*, 94–5).

Allen met the political agent for Dadur, Major James Outram, a friend from Karachi. One night at his dinner table there was a lively discussion about how the disaster at Kabul could possibly have happened without some prior knowledge of the revolt coming to the British. Many ingenious theories were advanced but 'none of them seemed very satisfactory'.

One week in Dadur was dominated by Hindu and Muslim religious festivals that made Allen feel very uncomfortable. Whilst he enjoyed the picturesque costumes and activities of the natives, on most occasions he was repelled by the incessantly beating drums, 'savage figures painted on naked flesh', 'dancing about with every kind of fantastic monkey trick' and his Hindu servants coming with painted foreheads to beg for money. He regretted that he could not speak their language fluently enough to tell them what he thought of such practices: it was probably just as well that he could not.

On 25 February Allen rode to Major Outram's camp to pay his respects to the young Khan of Kalat, a useful ally who had recently joined the British and who, it was hoped, would safeguard the army's rear during its further incursions into Afghanistan. Allen was to be presented as a *mullah* (the nearest job description to his calling that the major could think of). They proceeded to the parade ground of the 41st where the guard presented arms and the band played in honour of the Khan. They then entered a tent where the Khan sat, European fashion, on a chair whilst most of his chiefs and nobles preferred the carpets. He was only seventeen but seemed older, probably due to the hard and unpredictable life that he had led. His hair fell in long, black ringlets and he wore loose trousers and a vest of crimson silk embroidered with gold and carried a shield and curved sword in a scabbard of the same colour. Allen thought that he seemed haughty and distrustful but admitted that this was understandable after the bad treatment he had, in the past, received from the British. The atmosphere in the tent was overpoweringly hot and when asked the traditional question, 'Are you happy?' by a dignitary at his feet, Allen felt that his response, the customary 'Perfectly happy' was being economical with the truth.

The desperate situation in Afghanistan made it a matter of urgency for General England to reach Kandahar as soon as he had assembled sufficient men and supplies. By early March 1842 the relief force was ready and Allen, still tormented by heat and flies, was delighted to leave: 'Dadur with the most unpleasing recollections, and sincerely thanked God that I was not destined to spend a hot season there [it could reach 130 degrees Fahrenheit]' (*Diary*, 101).

CHAPTER 2

Through the Passes to Kandahar

Once the Reverend Allen left Dadur he became part of the force that was to relieve General Nott at Kandahar and, eventually as 'the army of retribution', fight its way through Afghanistan to join with General Pollock at Kabul. The only serious losses that were sustained at this early stage occurred when General England tried to get through the Khojuk pass with insufficient support and retired with heavy casualties. Allen was not obliged to accompany him on his second, successful attempt but he did so out of a love of adventure and a feeling that it was his duty to minister to the European soldiers.

Allen had not been involved in any fighting during his journey from India through Sind but all that was to change once England's brigade reached Baluchistan, a dangerous frontier area. Some British allies were prepared to give assistance but several local chiefs hated the 'infidels' and were delighted by the news of their defeat near Kabul in January. Akbar Khan did not have much influence in the area over the border, in Helmand and at Kandahar, but he was scared that Nott would be reinforced by the men, supplies and treasure that would enable him to march on Kabul. He was no soft touch like Elphinstone and Akbar shared his anxiety with the prisoners that, if taken, he would either be hung or blown from a gun (see Part I, Chapter 6). A renegade son of Shah Shujah, Sufter Jung, in league with some local chiefs, hoped to take Kandahar for himself and was prepared to fight for it. England, an indifferent commander, now had to run the gauntlet of the hostile tribesmen in the Bolan and Khojuk passes before he could reach that city.

The force moved off from Dadur soon after 2.00 am on 7 March taking grain, fodder and even firewood for cooking with them as the terrain they were to cross was utterly barren. Allen by that time had nine camels to carry all the supplies for himself and his servants as well as his vestments, other religious articles and his precious books. It was a relief to reach the Bolan pass for, although the sun was very hot, there was a clear stream and shade to be had under the rocks: 'I could not forbear remarking to a companion near me, the beautiful illustration we had during our march of the force of the scripture metaphor, "As rivers of water in a dry place, as the shadow of a great rock in a weary land"' (Isaiah, xxxii, 2) (*Diary*, 104). They arrived at their camp at Kundye at 9.00 am after marching for about 11 miles and were pleased to find that, although it was still hot, there was a cool breeze, no dust and few flies.

The following morning the force left early again and marched through beautiful but dangerous steep rocks, crossing and re-crossing a stream, it was a notorious spot for sniper fire and everyone was apprehensive. When nothing happened Allen heard men of the 41st saying to each other: '"What fools these people must be to let us into their country, when they have such a pass as this!"' (*Diary*, 106). They arrived at Gurm-ab (warm spring) where the pass was about a mile wide and they could make their camp in relative security.

The next day, 9 March, they travelled 11 miles to Beebeenanee which took its name from a lady pursued by giants 'with evil designs'. She begged the mountains to save her and they obliged by opening up a cave into which she escaped. When they arrived it was so hot that Allen and two other officers sheltered under an ammunition cart, he sat on his cloak and made a good breakfast of cold beef. He felt that people in England would think this was undignified behaviour but professed himself to be 'tolerably comfortable'.

The force endured a very difficult journey to Abegoom on 10 March through deep layers of stones and shingle that tormented the cattle, especially the bullocks. The road was much steeper than before which increased their difficulties and the feet of some of the unshod ponies began to bleed. The prevailing misery was not alleviated by the sight of the tomb of Mrs Smith when they stopped: she was the conductor's wife who had been murdered the previous year (see Part I, Chapter 1). Some of the soldiers of the 41st set to work and plastered and repaired the tomb and most men went to pay their respects to it in the course of the day. Allen was disgusted by the fact that the bandit who was thought to have done the deed was with the force being paid to act as a guide.

General England has not enjoyed a high reputation as a leader and his failings were brought out through Allen's apprehensions about their next campsite at Sir-i-Bolan. It looked as if it was going to rain but the camp was situated in the unstable bed of a river exactly where in the previous year a party from Bengal had lost all their baggage, cattle and forty-five people in a flash flood. Allen did not explicitly criticise England but his choice of a site was rash and they were fortunate, in the event, not to have been troubled by rain. On their way to the camp, it was Allen's turn to be rash: with one officer and a few followers he left the main body believing that they were making a short cut. For a while they lost sight of the main column and feared that they might be attacked by robbers. They were relieved eventually to rejoin the rest of the army but they had taken a foolish risk since Allen's *Diary* is full of tales of stragglers and wanderers who got their throats cut.

The brigade had to spend three days at the unpromising campsite since during the first night a fierce, cold wind started blowing. Allen had to rouse his servants several times to prevent the tents from blowing away (they had a separate, smaller one). The camels had suffered so it was decided to stay put the following day: Allen wrapped himself, his servants and animals in all available rugs and cloths to protect them from the wind, hot tea and brandy-water also fortified the humans. The bad weather continued on Sunday 13 March so they stayed where they were. Everyone suffered from cracked and blistered lips and the camels and bullocks were dying in large numbers, but Allen thanked God that at least there was no rain or snow. The troops could not be assembled in the open air so he celebrated divine service in his tent, it was well filled and General England attended.

The wind had subsided by 14 March so the journey continued through the most dangerous part of the pass. The British called it 'the Zig-Zags' because the narrow, rocky defile made several sharp, angular turns, sometimes giving the impression that they were approaching a blank wall. It was a perfect place for an ambush and a friend of Allen's had been attacked there in the previous year. On this occasion Major Boyd, the quarter-master general, crowned the heights on the right-hand side with 150 men before the main force set off. Everyone was alert straining 'to discover *puggerees* [turbans] and matchlocks among the stones' and had the uneasy feeling that they were being watched. Major Boyd dispersed a small body of Kaukers (tribesmen) from the heights and a private in the rear-guard had a lucky escape. He had wandered away and was pounced on and restrained and would probably have been killed if his fellows had not reached him in time and scared away his captors. When they had left the most dangerous part, Allen and a friend sat under a rock and ate a substantial *tiffin*, 'I have seldom enjoyed a luncheon more'.

The brigade emerged into a wide plain, Dusht-i-Bedoulut (the plain of poverty): since it was waterless they had brought a supply with them. Allen retired to bed relieved that no one had been killed in the pass. On the following day they marched into another plain covered with southern-wood which gave off an overpowering fragrance. The temperature had dropped, there was ice in the puddles and the great peak of Tukkatoo was covered with snow.

Allen and Major Boyd with a few horsemen rode in advance of the force on 16 March. The major pointed out several small, fortified villages inhabited by Sayeds who claimed to be direct descendants of the Prophet. They were venerated and their blessings or curses were taken very seriously by believers; they even claimed that they could render British guns harmless. Allen's party was later alarmed to encounter an imposing and heavily armed body of horsemen but they received a friendly greeting from them. It was a chief and his retinue from Mastung coming to pay his respects to one of the senior officers. When asked, on this occasion, Allen could genuinely reply to his interlocutor that he was very happy.

England's brigade rode on to Quetta, in Baluchistan, which proved to be a most attractive town in the fertile, well-watered valley of Shaul. The residency and *cantonments* of the 20th Bengal Regiment Native Infantry were a little way out of the town and had recently been hastily fortified, as an attack by hostile Baluchis was expected: the defences were strengthened by a ditch and a 7ft wall. Despite the cold, apricot trees were blooming and a small blue iris covered the ground: this flower was unfortunately fatal to about thirty bullocks and also disagreed with the horses. Allen and Boyd were offered hospitality by Major Apthorpe of the 20th, a soldier who was admired for his gallantry. The chaplain could not imagine that in less than a fortnight, due to the evil fortunes of war, he would be burying this fine officer.

Forage was scarce around Quetta so General England took his force towards Killa-ab-Doolah, 5 miles up the Pisheen valley. Allen did not realise that the general actually intended to push on to Kandahar so he decided to stay in Quetta for the time being to see what would happen. He bought a little house from an officer, it was very simple but he delighted in its fireplace and a glass window, so he could keep both cold and dust at bay. He held two services every Sunday and administered Holy Communion to seven people on Easter Day on 27 March. Good news arrived that Colonel Lane had won a victory against huge odds at Kandahar on 10 March whilst General Nott was absent on a punitive expedition. The Afghans seem to have tried to lure the whole army away from the city so that they could take it but failed in the face of the small but resolute defending force.

To his dismay Allen heard that General England's force had been halted by strong resistance on 28 March at Haikalzai. The enemy had thrown a breastwork between two hills near the entry to the Khojuk pass and fired down on England's force from the heights. Captain May, commanding a light company of the 41st in the advance, was shot dead (his body was not recovered) and several of his men were killed or wounded. As the British retreated Major Apthorpe was mortally wounded: they retired to a ruined fort where they bivouacked for the night in heavy rain. The next day they managed to retreat in good order and reached Quetta on 31 March, bringing Apthorpe's body with them; twenty-six altogether had been killed and sixty-nine wounded. His sepoys visited the major's body with many tears and groans and the following morning it was buried by Allen in the presence of a large number of officers and the whole light battalion.

The Indian papers, according to Allen, made a meal of the reverse and quite unfairly blamed the sepoys for the defeat: alarm spread throughout India and the Afghans were encouraged to continue to resist. Norris (395) thought that the principal responsibility for the defeat must rest with England who pushed on to the dangerous pass without waiting for the rest of his brigade to arrive at Quetta: Allen certainly does not seem to have known what his intentions were. England might have assumed that Nott would send a force from Kandahar to meet him half way but seems to have done nothing to arrange for this to happen. If the British Army should have learnt one thing from the disaster of January it was that, when going through passes in Afghanistan, it was essential to crown the heights, and this England had failed to do. The newly published *Illustrated London News* certainly blamed him, writing with heavy irony:

> General England seems to have lost all hope for the present of forwarding troops to Candahar, the brigade destined for its reinforcement now being considered necessary at Quettah, where strong intrenchments are being thrown up. We do not quite comprehend the reason for this sudden alteration in General England's resolution; as there seems to have occurred no such change in the state of the Shawl country, betwixt the 28th of March and the 1st April, as to make the presence of 2500 men, which at the former date were partly on their way to reinforce General Nott, necessary at the latter one for the protection of Quettah.
>
> (11 June 1842, 69)

Quetta was on the border of Afghanistan and the British were subjected to minor harassment from the enemy, for example, a female grass-cutter had her throat cut only a quarter of a mile from the camp. A force, including Allen's friend Captain Stuart, arrived from Dadur on 4 April which had managed to get through the Bolan pass without casualties. The brigade now numbered nearly 3,000 men plus their servants and camp followers, conditions were very crowded and, according to the medical officers, dangerously insanitary. News came on 23 April that Shah Shujah had been murdered in Kabul: as the British had originally entered Afghanistan as his agents to effect his restoration, the legal basis for the garrisons at Kandahar and Jalalabad was now debatable.

General Nott was untroubled by such legal niceties and he wrote peremptorily to General England ordering him to advance to Kandahar immediately. He wished to spare Allen the dangers of the journey but the clergyman felt that, as nearly all the European soldiers were going, it was his duty to accompany them, and he admitted that: 'a strong feeling of curiosity and desire of travel which I had felt from childhood, impelled me forward' (*Diary*, 129).

This time England had arranged with Nott that he would arrive at the southern end of the Khojuk pass by 1 May and a brigade from Kandahar would await him at the northern end. Allen was in some difficulty as he had sold all his camels but he managed to acquire four, less than half those he had used to get to Quetta. This meant that he had to sacrifice his beloved books since clothes, food and liquors were indispensable (he did not mention camping gear but he still had tents and bedding). He wrote that, apart from the books, it was remarkable how little he missed his other possessions. On the previous Sunday, after the other services, he and a few officers had met for a 'social prayer' to beg for God's blessing on the expedition.

The brigade left on 26 April whilst it was still dark but when daylight came Allen appreciated the beauty of the view back to Quetta and the rocks covered with wild flowers such as red poppies. His reaction to Afghan scenery may be compared with Lady Sale's enthusiasm: she was a gardener, he was an artist and both spent much time being cooped up, she as a prisoner, while for Allen it was often dangerous to wander, so they both showed a lively appreciation for nature when they were travelling.

The heat of the sun was overpowering and the brigade was relieved to reach the camp and some shade at Kuchlak, spending their first night in Afghanistan. Allen had been so badly affected by the sun that he became dizzy and bilious and had to ride in a litter on the following day when they reached Hyderzye. The green wheat in this part of the valley that led to the pass provided welcome forage: Allen evidently felt badly about the army taking the locals' crops but observed that, even had they wished to pay for them, everyone had fled. The locals tried to take revenge by tempting the camel men to give them some of their animals but prompt action by the cavalry foiled their plan. The next day, 28 April, was exactly a month after England's defeat at Haikalzai and Allen prayed earnestly that either action would be averted or that the British would be victorious.

The brigade continued to march up the Kuchlack valley and, at 7.00 am, reached Haikalzai, the heights were bristling with Afghans, their flags were flying and horsemen were galloping about. The low hills increased in height until they reached the pass and the first and lowest on the right was used as a depot for the army's treasure, ammunition and baggage camels, protected by the foot artillery and and companies of native artillery. Allen observed the action from that vantage point with his spy-glass. The Bengal artillery, Captain Leslie's Bombay horse artillery and the reserve occupied the centre, whilst guns under Lieutenant Brett were sent to the low hills on the left. At 7.30 am Leslie and Brett opened fire on the enemy in the hills; at first they shot too low but, when that had been corrected, caused considerable confusion. Under cover of Brett's fire, a party of European and native troops led by Major Simmonds, advanced up the low hills, crossed the ravines, gained the heights and chased off the Afghans. Allen believed that the cavalry might have cut off their retreat and killed sufficient Afghans to prevent 'further mischief' but his Christian relief that there were so few casualties soon triumphed over his disappointment. The enemy horsemen fled as soon as they saw that the heights were crowned with the result that there were no deaths on the British side and very few wounded. It was usually impossible to estimate Afghan casualties accurately as they took away their dead and wounded. Allen rode up to the hill that had recently been held by the enemy and congratulated his friends with tears of joy in his eyes.

As Allen went through the pass he saw a crowd standing round the body of an elderly Afghan who had just been shot. He had fought bravely with his spear until he was killed but, when the clergyman expressed pity for him, the others rejected his feelings disdainfully. This led him to make the general point that Afghans would attack weak or defenceless foes but avoid conflict with equals, yet if they were cornered like the old man, they would fight bravely to the last. This was the first occasion on which Allen had been involved in an armed conflict and he surprised himself by his reaction to it:

> If anyone had asked me, when on a quiet curacy in England, how I expected to feel under such circumstances, my reliance on my own heroism was so small, that I should certainly have expressed my wish to be anywhere else than amidst such a scene. I was not, however, now sensible of any such feeling; on the contrary, I had a strong desire to press forward and see the worst; a desire, by-the-bye, which was afterwards accomplished in a more considerable affair.
>
> (*Diary*, 144–5)

He conceded that many would feel apprehensions before an engagement but not once it had started and he observed that this was also the case with young recruits just arrived from Britain who, like himself, had never been in battle.

The brigade camped near Haikalzai and Allen was again concerned for the peasants whose fields of growing wheat were trampled and devoured by thousands of camels, horses, ponies and bullocks, 'but such are the miseries of war'. The camp followers plundered the town and set it alight so it was almost entirely destroyed. In the evening Allen conducted a burial service over the mangled remains of eighteen bodies left from the previous action that had been attacked by jackals, *pariah* dogs and kites: 'Captain May was identified by his profuse blond hair. The whole regiment of the 41st that was off duty and a large number of officers attended: Man that is born of a woman hath but a short time to live, and is full of misery; he cometh up, and is cut down like a flower' (*Diary*, 147).

Undeterred by their defeat parties of the enemy hung on the brigade's rear and, on 30 April, Allen was distressed to lose one of his camel men. He had been sickly and lagged behind and no one knew exactly what happened but he was never seen again. That day they camped near the fort of Killa-ab-Doolah and received the submission of its owner who had been fighting them at Haikalzai, as it was accepted he saved his property. One of the refrains of the *Diary* was pity for innocent villagers caught up in a conflict that was not of their making. The desolation caused by an Asian army was not so much from the fighting or even the pillaging by soldiers but by the needs of large numbers of cattle and draught animals and the camp followers who tended them.

Sunday 1 May caused Allen's thoughts to turn to home and particularly the celebrations on that day, but it was also pleasant for everyone in the camp as they were allowed to halt and enjoy the good water that flowed at Killa. The enemy horse were still in the hills and shots were fired from time to time but no harm was done. In the middle of the day a messenger arrived from Brigadier Wymer, he was at the northern entrance to the Khojuk pass and would co-operate with England's force on the following day. They also heard the good news of General Sale's victory over Akbar Khan at Jalalabad on 7 April. The distances involved meant that the other good news from that town, General Pollock's arrival with his relief force on 15 April, was not then known. In the cool of the evening the European troops were drawn up in a square and Allen celebrated a service that was even attended by some Roman Catholics.

The force was assembled at 4.00 am on the following day. Although there were still groups of Afghans on the peaks above them, the lower hills had been secured, so their fire did little damage either to the column or to the baggage and only two men were slightly wounded. Allen was sufficiently relaxed to admire the scenery that was 'exceedingly pretty' and reminded him of parts of northern England. The road was so narrow that it soon became jammed with camels, so he philosophically sat under a shady rock and breakfasted on cold beef and eggs. He then rode further on to the steep ascent of the pass and looking up saw Wymer crowning the heights: an achievement paid for by two lives and several men wounded. At the top of a ridge the road divided into two, both narrow ways, the guns were dragged manually along one and the camels and bullocks were led along the other. A number fell under their loads and had to be destroyed, making the way even harder to negotiate. It was time for *tiffin* and Allen happily joined a group of officers eating from a litter well supplied with beef, tongue etc.: the constant deaths of bullocks at least ensured that those fresh foods were never in short supply. Hindu sepoys preferred not to eat any kind of beef but sometimes, when nothing else was available, some of them had to, calling it 'red mutton'.

Allen later rode down the road used by the guns to the plain below and arrived at the camp at Chummun at 5.00 pm. He had been on the road for more than twelve hours but some of the officers and men crowning the heights had been on duty for twenty-four hours, much of it in the burning sun. Allen found a mess tent that had already been erected and threw himself into its shade and slept there until dinner time. Afterwards he was relieved to find that his camels had arrived and telling his servants to pitch his tent he slept again, without unpacking, until broad daylight. The force had come through the Khojuk pass with few losses and this was largely due to Wymer who had crowned the heights at its exit, although England had done the same at the earlier stages. Care had been taken to regulate the always potentially lethal mixture of ungainly, burdened animals and large numbers of followers. If the former fell they were shot and quickly cleared out of the way. The obstacles experienced during the retreat from Kabul in January had been much greater: the snow and the starvation of men and beasts, but the main problem had been the lack of military discipline and leadership.

On 3 May everyone rested and Allen took the opportunity to view the Bengal troops led by Brigadier Wymer. They were very fine, tall and well made in comparison to the Bombay troops he knew and he was particularly impressed with the Shah's irregular cavalry in their crimson dresses. There was little wildlife for him to observe in his leisure hours apart from a few lizards and dung beetles whose antics he enjoyed, although he did later kill a small, white scorpion in his tent. The following day, after dinner, the force set out at 5.30 pm to avoid the heat. Allen rode with the advance of the 3rd Bombay cavalry but they soon halted as the now enormous baggage train of the combined brigades caused confusion by closing in on both flanks. When they eventually moved on Allen commented on the 'picturesque appearance of the line of march of an Indian army'. He soon felt very tired and was glad to sleep on the ground for an hour, wrapped up in his coat: 'I thought neither of rheumatism, fever, nor snakes, all of which would probably have troubled my mind a month ago' (*Diary*, 162). They started off again and one of the officers was entertaining them by singing 'The Mistletoe Bough' when someone fired on them from the thick vegetation, but they were so accustomed to such shots by that time that he just continued his song. At 2.00 am the servants made a little fire and supper was served from a litter.

Everyone was exhausted by the time that they reached their camp at Kolgie but there was to be no rest. A hot wind blew, throwing up clouds of dust that penetrated everywhere: into Allen's pen, on his paper and spectacles so he could neither read nor write. He tried to sleep but discomfort from the dust prevented him, in the end he sat with his eyes closed with a handkerchief over his head. The dust storm, unusually, continued blowing after dark: even the water there was 'brackish and bad'.

The march for the next two days proved tedious and was without incident as Allen morosely remarked: 'It seemed scarcely possible to conceive any other country where one could travel so far and see so little of interest' (*Diary*, 165). There was a rumour that Sufter Jung, the renegade son of Shah Shujah, would attack and a few shots were fired during the night of 7 May but no harm was done. At this time Allen was reflecting on the probable sufferings of the prisoners and calling to mind one of the petitions from the Litany for all prisoners and captives which: 'became invested with an interest in my mind which it never possessed before' (*Diary*, 166).

They marched 11 miles to Deh Hajee on Sunday 8 May where a shortage of timber had led to the construction of small, domed houses made of sun-dried brick. Their courtyards and mulberry trees made them a pleasing sight but they were completely deserted. Captain Leslie offered his spacious quarters in what might have been a mosque for divine service but it alarmed the 'sensitive nerves of a political agent' and General England refused permission on the grounds that it might offend the locals. Allen was reduced to the restricted space of the hot mess tent and indignantly protested to his *Diary* that it was scarcely logical to worry about local feelings when the place was empty and the army had habitually been killing Afghans, burning their villages and plundering their crops.

The next camp on 9 May was in a fine valley at Khoosh-ab which was cultivated with wheat and in full view of Kandahar. The local chief was friendly so the final stage in this journey was pleasant and relatively free of danger. On its second attempt the brigade had come from Quetta without serious casualties, although Colonel Wymer had lost two men when he met them at the Khojuk pass. Good weather had arrived and, even with its inflated numbers (approximately 10,000) Nott's domination of the countryside enabled him to feed the force, its camp followers and beasts for some time. This was just as well as it had to remain there for several months whilst Lord Ellenborough made up his mind about whether they should withdraw to India or march on Kabul to punish the Afghans and rescue the prisoners.

CHAPTER 3

Kandahar, 'An Abundance of Lettuces'

The three months that the Reverend Allen spent at Kandahar provided a respite from the discomforts and dangers of the march from Sind. The heat was very trying, although we do not hear of the large number of illnesses and deaths that it certainly caused amongst Pollock's force in Jalalabad and the prisoners at Kabul. When Governor General Ellenborough finally made up his mind and allowed his generals to converge on Kabul, the formidable General Nott led a well-supplied army with high morale out of Kandahar.

General England not only brought reinforcements to Kandahar, he also provided much-needed supplies and treasure: stocks of ammunition were low and the troops had not been paid for several months. The town had not actually been under siege but it was near several hostile tribes, some of them supporters of Sufter Jung, so it was always dangerous to venture out of the city. Major Henry Rawlinson, the political agent, had strengthened security in early March by evicting about 5,000 men, women and children choosing those who were most likely to rise up against the British. This was a harsh measure but recent experience in Kabul made it a wise one and General Nott supported the policy. He got on well with Rawlinson, quite an achievement on the agent's part with such an irascible general. The garrison had levelled a large number of trees and other obstacles around the city to deprive attackers of cover, although the gardens, full of fruit and vegetables, survived. The garrison had done their best to make themselves comfortable: Knox records that the officers made an impromptu squash court against the wall of the mess house, using cricket bats instead of rackets but he admitted that they got extremely hot when they were playing.

On his arrival in Kandahar on 9 May Allen joined the mess of HM 40th Regiment of Foot who shared the *cantonments* with the 2nd and 16th Bengal Regiments Native Infantry, while the rest of the army was stationed in the town. Allen had originally been ordered to go and join the 40th back in Bombay a year before and had travelled with some of them up the Indus and he was now to become 'embedded'. As the only chaplain with the army, however, he also carried out religious duties for other regiments and enjoyed socialising with their officers. In his dedication and at the beginning of his chapter on Kandahar he wrote warmly of the courage and fortitude of the 40th but he feared that: 'their privations and exploits were by no means fully appreciated, for owing to the exceeding brevity of General Nott's dispatches, they had not the advantage of having them made known to the world' (*Diary*, 173). This sounds rather like discontented mess-table talk: Nott was respected and feared but little loved, except perhaps by his sepoys for whom he had a soft spot, he was colonel of the 42nd Bengal Regiment Native Infantry.

After remaining for four days in camp Allen was quartered, on the general's orders, in a charming house about a mile away in the city. He had some initial difficulty in gaining possession as its Afghan occupants were still there and unwilling to leave. Since it was already dusk he ordered his servants to clear one room and installed himself (rather risky – his throat might have been cut in the night). He applied to the police magistrate either to evict them or to give him another house but, on the third day, he returned from a ride to find that they were gone. His servants explained that Allen had arrived without warning and taken the room where the family had hidden all their treasure: gold, silver and rings under the threshold and in the walls. When they were sure that he was safely out of the way they had removed them and left for another of their houses.

Allen was delighted with his new home, a welcome change from his small tent; he was to stay there for three months, and with his artist's eye for detail, described it enthusiastically. There was an outer courtyard with a large stable, a prayer niche and a room for a *fakir* (holy beggar, elsewhere

Allen described them as 'idle, dirty and ragged'). Three living rooms, one with a high pointed arch was open on one side, all gave onto an inner court and were plastered in white and decorated with patterns of wreaths and flowers and covered in glittering talc (powdered talchum that has a glassy sheen). The kitchen and upstairs bedrooms occupied the other side of the courtyard, which contained a well of delicious water and a luxuriant vine. Allen needed some furniture and, not knowing how long he was going to be in Kandahar, improvised. Four stakes were driven into the earthen floor and the doors to the outer court, which were not required, were fixed on top. The result was rather rough and uneven but, when covered with a thick Persian carpet, it made a good table and was the site of 'many little parties' hosted by the convivial clergyman. The diet was more varied than it had been on the march, the city: 'furnished abundance of lettuces, and other fresh vegetables, from which we found much benefit, having been for a long time living almost entirely on animal food' (*Diary*, 174).

Kandahar was entirely enclosed by walls, over 3 miles in extent and of varying thickness (Illustration 14). Allen and his friends took their morning and evening strolls on the ramparts, enjoying the extensive view since it was too hot to walk about in the middle of the day and too dangerous to venture out of the city. In the centre there were four wide bazaars, one led to a large square containing the citadel which bristled with captured native guns as well as British six-, nine- and eighteen-pounders. When they walked in the streets Allen found the scenes of men in flowing garments prostrating themselves in prayer positively biblical. He admired the fervour of their worship, contrasting it with the 'timidity and shame of Christians in the avowal of their faith' but regretted Muslim 'erroneous direction'.

The bazaars fascinated Allen and the way in which different areas specialised in particular products: *poshteens*; silks, cashmir shawls and linens; hardware from as far afield as St Petersburg and Birmingham; cooked meat stalls and sellers of little birds in wicker cages. Poets and storytellers attracted appreciative audiences who were rapt by their noisy recitations accompanied by violent gestures. Blind beggars, rampaging children and a few heavily veiled women all added to the picturesque scene. Allen was amused by the antics of the *pariah* dogs who liked to climb to the top of houses and even to their domes to enjoy the coolest breezes. He had heard that good shampoos could be obtained in the public baths but could not bring himself to try one on the excuse that they might not be clean.

The fine octagonal, domed tomb of Ahmed Shah, founder of the Durrani monarchy (ancestor of both Dost Mohammed and Shah Shujah) stood in a corner of the city. Generally, Allen was sensitive to local susceptibilities but one passage from his *Diary* was ominous for future understanding between the Afghans and their British invaders:

> In former days no one could enter this shrine without putting off his shoes; now, however, we do as we like, and since we take off our hats, which they well know is our method of showing respect, they ought not to take offence, we always being content with their putting off their shoes, and never requiring them to uncover the head in showing respect to us or our habitations.

(Diary, 190)

On Sunday mornings during his stay Allen celebrated services alternately for the 40th and 41st. In the afternoon he had two double-poled tents pitched in the citadel for the artillery and some officers and was gratified to see increasing numbers of the latter attend despite the heat (up to 137 degrees), wind and dust. On 19 May a strong brigade under Brigadier Wymer that included the 40th and Captain Leslie's horse artillery marched to the relief of the small garrison at Kalat-i-Ghilzai. Whilst they were on their way Kalat was attacked 'with great ferocity' but Captain Craigie, its commander, repulsed the enemy causing heavy casualties. Nott and Rawlinson had decided to abandon the fortress so the defences were destroyed before the brigade returned to Kandahar. It was still to be some time before Ellenborough decided whether he would withdraw all his forces or send them to Kabul. Nott, ever careful of his men and remembering the fall of Ghazni, probably wanted to save the defenders of Kalat from such a fate.

The departure of Wymer for Kalat deluded Sufter Jung and his allies into believing that Kandahar was sufficiently weakened for them to risk an attack. Threatening bodies of horsemen were observed on several occasions, once on a Sunday, disrupting Allen's services to his intense irritation. On 27 May he accompanied General England and his staff on a visit to one of Shah Shujah's good sons, the eldest, Timur Shah, who was recognised by some as king: he had a gentle, peaceable temperament and was, therefore, despised by the Afghans. He was afraid of meeting his father's fate and had proclaimed his intention of remaining with the British army remembering, no doubt, his previous comfortable exile in India. He occupied beautiful apartments in the palace built by Ahmed Shah, 'more completely oriental than anything I had previously seen'. The general and his party were all seated on chairs, on a costly carpet from Herat by a tranquil pool in a courtyard; Rawlinson, who spoke Persian, interpreted. The Shah was richly dressed, rather fat and resembled, Allen was told, his late father: the clergyman liked his serious and dignified manner that was devoid of pride. He expressed his regret that he had never learnt English as a youth, he had since tried but had not made much progress. His two sons were introduced, they were boys of twelve and nine, who were more warlike in their tastes than their father and Allen was not optimistic about how they would develop.

The threatened attack by Sufter Jung and his allies came on another Sunday, 29 May, outside Kandahar at Baba Wullee. Nott turned out the 41st, two regiments of native infantry, some artillery and such cavalry as had not gone to Kalat. Allen rode to one of the city gates and observed three large bodies of enemy cavalry on some low hills about a mile and a half away. They were firing at the Shah's artillery that was responding vigorously but Allen could not see all the action because much was hidden by the gardens between them and the town. The Afghan horsemen recoiled from the fire but took possession of a village although they were unable to keep it for long and by 3.00 pm were in retreat. It was estimated that there had been about 5,000 assailants, mainly horse, and that about 200 had been killed and 200 wounded. On the British side two or three sepoys had been killed and Lieutenants Chamberlayne and Mainwaring (a different officer from the prisoner, Mrs Mainwaring's husband, who was in Jalalabad) were wounded. Allen did not give the number of troops, European or native, who were wounded but he later said that he visited seven from the 41st in hospital.

117

The success of the British action was partially due to the bravery of 200 Persian horsemen led by their prince, Aga Mohammed Khan, reputed to be the leader of the Assassins (a fanatical Shia sect that appeared in Syria and Persia in the eleventh century AD) and a descendant of the legendary Old Man of the Mountain. Sufter Jung was present at the action but shortly afterwards he submitted to General Nott and was treated, according to Allen, 'with greater leniency than he deserved'. Also present was the mother of the rebellious chief who had been blown from a gun the previous October (see Part I, Chapter 1): 'This lady pretended to a vision of the prophet, and was playing Joan of Arc among the Affghans' (*Diary*, 198).

During the following week when Allen was visiting the wounded he was impressed by their cheerfulness and good humour. One lad had taken a little piece of lead in the calf of his leg which he produced saying disparagingly to Allen's amusement: 'it's hardly worth calling a ball . . . You see, sir . . . poor creatures! – they've no way of hitting 'em together; they don't run 'em, as we do. Why one of our balls would make half-a-dozen of 'em' (*Diary*, 200).

In early June Allen was invited by an officer, who spoke Persian and could interpret, to dine with Aga Mohammed and he was pleased to have a chance to experience Eastern manners. They were received in an open court and joined the prince on a raised platform: he sat on a couch that also served as a table but, as Europeans, they were given chairs (this proved to be their undoing). A few snacks were placed on the couch and their host enquired: 'what could have brought the *Feringhee moollah* so far, whether he drank wine etc.; good-humouredly expressed dissatisfaction at the scantiness of my beard, and seemed rather shocked that a person of such sacred character should caress a spaniel dog that was paying his court to the company [dogs are considered unclean by many Muslims]' (*Diary*, 202). Obviously relieved that strong drinks did not offend the *mullah*, the prince enthusiastically drank a quantity of very inferior wine and spirits (all that could be had in Kandahar).

The familiar behaviour of the servants disgusted Allen for they chatted and helped themselves liberally to the food before it reached the guests. A *hookah* (pipe) was passed round and some, but clearly not Allen, took a few whiffs. The prince offered some music and a 'wild-looking man' produced a small guitar but needed some opium before he could play it. He was joined by a singer and they started to perform but Allen was warned that it was not proper etiquette to listen attentively. He thought that the tunes were attractive but was not impressed by the quality of their performance. Water was brought to wash their hands then a large number of dishes of meat, eggs and other foods were served on the couch without order and the guests used large, flat cakes that served the triple function of bread, plate and napkin. Allen found that it was very difficult to bend down from his chair to convey food with his hands to his mouth from the couch. In the end he abandoned it and sat 'cross-legged, tailor-wise' on the platform so his face was near the couch. He was relieved when his hands were again washed, tea was served, the *hookah* circulated and they could depart.

The extreme heat kept Allen indoors for much of the time, a trial for him as he was an active, sociable man and also missed his books. His main activities, apart from strolling around the city, were Sunday services, visiting the sick and occasionally spending a day with the 40th at the *cantonments*. When he was there he could inspect the schools that were held for both adults and children. He examined the boys on the scriptures and catechism and was pleased to find that their standards were as high as they would have been in Bombay or Poona. He commended the regiment's practice of requiring each NCO to pass an examination in a higher branch of arithmetic before they could achieve further promotion. This produced 'respectable and well-conducted' officers, diminished drunkenness and disorder and was probably the reason why no corporal punishment was administered whilst Allen was with the regiment. The good discipline that prevailed was also demonstrated by the attentiveness of the men during the services he celebrated. He had shortened them in recognition that the troops had to stand in the heat and that, if it became an ordeal, it would be counterproductive; in the evenings he held a full service in a tent for the officers. He and they were often struck by the parallels between the scriptures and what they experienced in Afghanistan. His lesson on 3 July, for example, referred to the poor man and his ewe lamb, and the peasants and sepoys often kept such animals as pets. Allen's horse-keeper bought one in Quetta which he decorated with orange dye and a necklace of ribbons and shells and which went everywhere with him.

In mid-July orders arrived that the forces levied in the name of the late Shah should be disbanded and activities in the commissariat and ordnance departments indicated that there would soon be a move but:

> none could divine what the government proposed to do with respect to the prisoners at Ghuznee and Kabul. All was kept a profound secret; and though the destruction of the fortress of Khelat-i-Ghilgie seemed to forbid the hope of advance, we could not bring ourselves to believe that it was the intention of government to withdraw through the Bolan, and abandon these unfortunate captives to their fate.

> (*Diary*, 208–9)

Allen and his fellow officers did not know that Lord Ellenborough had written to Nott at Kandahar on 4 July ordering him to retreat from Afghanistan but giving him the option of doing so either via the passes that led directly to India or via Kabul and that this was copied to Pollock (Kaye, vol. 3, 288). Kaye was scornful of the cowardly way in which the Governor General put the responsibility for taking such a decision onto his generals but, resolute and able as they both were, they privately agreed to converge on Kabul.

On 26 July the officers of the 3rd Cavalry invited Allen to join them for a picnic at Baba Wullee, a village about 6 miles from Kandahar on the banks of the Urghundab river. One of his particular friends, Captain Reeves, was his host and officers from other regiments also accompanied them along with an escort of 100 of Skinner's horse, so dangerous was the area. After riding down a beautiful valley they pitched a tent in a mulberry grove near the ruined hall of Baba Wullee, who was reputed to have been a giant. Some of them fished, others went shooting, chatted, slept or, in Allen's case, sketched. They ate the excellent fish that they had caught for dinner and gathered mulberries and magnificent peaches from a nearby garden. Allen greatly enjoyed the day after his long, hot confinement in Kandahar but, in retrospect, he was saddened by the fact that three of his companions, including Reeves, were soon to be killed.

Preparations for the evacuation of Kandahar were well under way: one part of the force under General England was to return to Sind via the Bolan pass. The other led by General Nott comprised 6,630 soldiers including nearly all the Europeans. Their destination was still a secret but the presence of heavy guns convinced everyone that they would be going at least as far as Ghazni. Allen asked Nott which force he should join and the general allowed him to make the decision himself. As in Quetta, Allen felt that he should minister to the Europeans so he decided to travel with Nott: 'I commended myself, therefore, to the providential care of God, not insensible to the probable perils of the expedition, yet feeling that I was in the execution of my duty; and I attribute it to his goodness that I had no uneasy apprehensions' (*Diary*, 213). He drew great satisfaction from a service of Holy Communion that he held a few days before their departure for members of all three Presidencies (Bengal, Madras and Bombay), some were going with England, some with Nott. He regretted that soldiers in the field who urgently needed the comforts of religion had few such opportunities. It is not clear whether he was blaming the British government, the Anglican Church or the army for that state of affairs.

As part of the preliminaries to leaving Kandahar, on 4 August, the superfluous ammunition had to be destroyed. The city was to be spared and was left under the rule of the nefarious Sufter Jung, 'to hold it if he could'. Allen said that a sergeant of artillery spread large numbers of ball cartridges over an enclosed courtyard and set fire to them causing a huge explosion. Several glass windows ('not very plentiful in Kandahar') were shattered, balls flew in all directions and a few people were burnt and bruised but no one was killed. Nott gave a more detailed account of the incident in a letter to his daughters:

> I have just been nearly sent out of the world. Some damaged powder, ammunition etc. which we intended to destroy, had been placed in what we called the Shah's magazine, where there was much warlike stuff belonging to the late King, also many shells. A fellow must needs take his stinking cigar into the place (I suppose he was drunk), and so set fire to the whole, and a very decent explosion took place. Two doors in my house were knocked to pieces. The shower of shot

121

came rattling against my house, and from fifteen to twenty musket balls were found in my room. I was involved in smoke and dust, and my escape was most providential.

(Stocqueler, vol. 2, 115–16)

Apart from the ammunition, nothing was destroyed in Kandahar so the unreliable Sufter Jung was left a defensible position.

At the end of Chapter 7 of Allen's *Diary*, where he had described his time in Kandahar, he paid tribute to General Nott's courage and resolution in undertaking the campaign to fight for Ghazni and then Kabul. He believed that it was not until after he had taken Ghazni that he knew for certain that General Pollock was advancing in the same direction. Nott's assurance to Ellenborough that he had sufficient resources of men and supplies to undertake the expedition was the principal reason for the Governor General's permission to advance. 'To him [Nott], under God, the gratitude of his country is mainly due for the restored stability of our empire in the East' (*Diary*, 215).

CHAPTER 4

The March to Ghazni

The fall of Ghazni in early September 1842 marked a defining stage in the punitive campaign. Thousands of Afghan horsemen and jezailchis were deployed against General Nott's army but they were swept aside with relatively light casualties. The British had no problem in obtaining supplies and, in the plains, the superior fire-power of their heavy guns and their good discipline proved decisive.

Once General Nott's army had left Kandahar on 7 August 1842, comfort and security were also left behind. We know with the benefit of hindsight that the expedition was to achieve limited success with acceptable levels of death and injury. At the time, however, the terrible fate of the remnants of the 'army of the Indus' early in the year must have been in everyone's mind. It was already August and it was to take over a month to reach Kabul – on a good day the army could cover 15 miles, the total distance was about 300 miles. Rest days, foraging and action against the enemy caused considerable delays. 'General Winter', the terrible Afghan weather, could close in towards the end of the year.

Lieutenant Knox, 42nd Bengal Regiment Native Infantry, quartermaster and interpreter, one of the officers who wrote a diary of the First Afghan War, gave a detailed account of Nott's force as it left Kandahar. There were twelve six-pounder guns divided between the Bombay and the late Shah's Horse Artilleries, a battery of six nine-pounders and a battery of four eighteen-pounders. Captain Delamaine commanded the 3rd Bombay Light Cavalry, Captain Haldane led the 1st Irregular Cavalry and Captain Christie commanded Christie's Horse, 1,060 cavalry altogether. The army was divided into two brigades, the first commanded by Brigadier Wymer was composed of Allen's regiment the 40th (650), the 16th Bombay Regiment

Native Infantry (750), the 38th Bengal Regiment Native Infantry (760) and the late Shah's 3rd Regiment Native Infantry (560). The second brigade was commanded by Brigadier Stacey and was composed of the 41st (600), the 2nd Bengal Regiment Native Infantry (750), the 42nd Bengal Regiment Native Infantry (750) and the 43rd Bengal Regiment Native Infantry (750), 6,630 men altogether. Amongst the officers with special duties the Reverend Allen is listed as 'padre' (*Nott's Brigade in Afghanistan*, 90–1). Majors Leech and Rawlinson were described as 'political agents', although Lord Ellenborough disliked the breed so much that he had stripped them of their powers. Nott, however, had a high regard for Rawlinson and appointed him as his aide-de-camp and continued to take his advice. Allen testified to the useful part Leech played in the campaign, especially in securing supplies.

Allen had shown considerable courage in choosing to remain as chaplain to the European soldiers rather than return to India with General England's force. His experiences between the Bolan pass and Kandahar had warned him that this was not to be the pleasant sightseeing trip that his early months on the journey through India had been: added to the inconveniences of dust, difficulties with camels and intense heat were the increasing dangers of enemy attack. His first problem occurred on 12 August on the march to Kul-i-Achool (the village of the schoolmaster) when he got entangled with the baggage cattle and lost a favourite terrier that he never saw again. He was heartened, however, by the sight of the army marching through fine country:

> the ground was prettily undulated, and the waving line of red uniforms, the cavalry, guns, and thousands of camels passing through it, was a striking contrast to the solitude around, and to the dark rocky hills rising on each side. This march brought us to the Turnuk River, passing through a valley, the verdure of which was exceedingly grateful to the eye accustomed to little but sterile rocks, and plains of dust and sand.
>
> (*Diary*, 220)

In the evening of Sunday 14 August Allen celebrated divine service in the mess tent of the 40th. The army marched in the mornings so he was to do this on every Sunday evening when circumstances permitted for there were to be no more prolonged rests until they reached Kabul. On this occasion he was disappointed by the low number of officers who attended, non-commissioned officers and privates never came as many were on duty, they had been marching all morning and no seats could be provided. When the killing started he noticed that attendance improved.

On 16 August the army marched 11 miles to Assia Huzara and Allen was concerned for the welfare of his horse-keeper who had been taken ill and lagged behind. He knew very well that stragglers were invariably butchered or sold as slaves by the locals but eventually the man turned up. Four sepoys of the 27th Bengal Regiment Native Infantry had joined the army since it left Kandahar. They were in poor condition having escaped from the servitude into which they had been reduced after the surrender of Ghazni. Allen was shocked by the bad treatment they received from their fellow Hindus who considered them unclean after their dealings with unbelievers. He strongly condemned the caste system that led to this and blamed foolish young European officers for colluding with it out of a mistaken sense of superiority. They failed to realise that high-caste Hindus despised them too! On this occasion, however, the European officers did set up a subscription for the relief of the escapees and any others who might appear.

The army marched to Kalat-i-Ghilzai on 17 August and viewed the ruins to which the fort had been reduced before the departure of the British occupying force in May. The locals seemed friendly despite that, selling the soldiers grain and straw, but two camel-men who strayed beyond the guard posts were murdered. Three days later at Nowruk Allen was shocked to find a crowd standing round a bush containing the bloodstained head of an Afghan who had been shot and then beheaded for trying to steal a camel. Allen mused on the biblical precedents for such barbarous behaviour. He also recalled an incident at Quetta, before his departure, when the commander of the Brahuis Horse proudly strode into the British residency during dinner, to display the severed head of an enemy. Allen concluded that all nations behaved violently in the excitement of action but that Christianity tended to moderate the cruelty of westerners.

The army reached Tazi on 21 August, the spot where the brigade under Colonel Maclaren sent by Nott from Kandahar to relieve Kabul was obliged to turn back in early December 1841 because, it was claimed, of the depth of the snow and the severity of the frost. The whole of their encampment was white with the bones of dead baggage cattle: shortage of draught animals might have been another reason for Maclaren's retreat (see Part I, Chapter 2). As time passed Nott's army was itself experiencing extremes of weather: near freezing at sunrise and over 100 degrees in the heat of the day but despite these rigours it remained remarkably healthy. So far the locals had been willing to sell them supplies, a circumstance that Allen attributed to the good offices of Major Leech.

As the army passed by other places where incidents in the war had taken place Allen mused: 'every spot told some tale of blood and slaughter, and the destruction of human life on both sides during the last four years, must have been much greater than is generally supposed' (*Diary*, 233). When the army approached Moquor on 27 August they feared that they would be attacked so they kept in close order. Three men were lost from the rear-guard when it was plundered but Nott was informed by Major Leech's messenger that 'his name had driven his foes away'. In fact, Shumshoodeen Khan, the chief who held Ghazni, fearing the British approach had raised all the local tribes against them and there was a little desultory firing on the camp but no one was hurt. Allen was more alarmed by a minor earthquake that disturbed him in bed during the night.

On 28 August the first serious engagement of the campaign took place after the army had marched 12 miles to Oba. The rear-guard had been harassed during the journey but they had killed about sixty of their assailants with a loss of five. Allen sent out a camel-man and groom with a foraging party from the camp but was then alarmed to hear that the grass-cutters were being slaughtered, the enemy were massing in great force for an attack and a body of cavalry was lost. A thick haze made it difficult to determine exactly what was happening: Captain Delamaine had taken out his horse troopers to investigate and destroyed a few enemy footmen and pursued the rest. When he arrived at a range of hills he and his men were fired on by large numbers of *jezailchis* from the heights, the cavalry tried to crown them but were thrown back with heavy casualties and they fled.

News of this disaster was brought to Nott, who was furious that Delamaine had acted without orders, and he mustered the whole army expecting to find a large force of Afghans to fight. The 'assembly' was sounded and the Bombay horse artillery under Captain Leslie and the light companies of infantry turned out. Allen accompanied Nott and his staff to the scene of action and on the outskirts of the camp they were relieved to see a confused body of camels, ponies and bullocks with their minders hurrying in (presumably these included Allen's servants, although he did not mention them). Behind rode the detachments of cavalry in good order but they had lost men, including Captains Bury and Reeves, the latter Allen's friend who had accompanied him on the picnic at Kandahar: the enemy, estimated to number about 5,000, sustained an equal loss.

Whilst the cavalry was recovering the bodies Nott went to a nearby village in a fort from where the initial attack on the grass-cutters was believed to have been made. He was met by unarmed villagers who begged for mercy and denied any involvement in the action, he told them to be quiet and sent Major Leech to look for evidence inside. He was met by a volley of matchlock balls and companies of the 40th and 41st with native troops stormed in. Resistance continued and every man they found was slaughtered; the women and children, a few of them wounded, were chased out: 'Seldom, I apprehend, has a clergyman looked on such a scene' (*Diary*, 241). Dead bodies were everywhere and the sepoys and followers were dragging out sheep, goats, oxen and goods. They also found a string of camels bearing the commissariat brand proving that the village had participated in the original attack on the grass-cutters. The fort was in flames and continued to burn all night. In all about 500 of the enemy had been killed while Nott lost 37 including the 2 officers.

Everyone was exhausted when they returned to camp as they had been in their saddles under the sun, including the march, for nearly ten hours but a further distressing task had to be completed. The headless remains of Captains Bury and Reeves were wrapped in their bedding and Allen sorrowfully presided over their burial together inside a tent. Straw was burnt on the site to disguise it as a watchfire in the hope that the locals would not find it and disinter the bodies as they were accustomed to do.

Allen then slept soundly after the exertions, dangers and calamities of the day.

For the next two days large numbers of Afghans followed the army beating their drums but they did little harm. When it arrived at its camp, Kara Barg (the Black Garden), on 30 August, they launched an attack from the fort of Goyain, a square tower with bastions at the angles, situated half a mile away. Nott, accompanied by Allen, turned out about 3,000 men and a strong artillery force to attack it. The Afghans were crowded onto the bastions firing their matchlocks and shouting defiance but apart from destroying the battlements of one bastion, the British guns did little damage. Lieutenant Terry of the Bombay artillery volunteered to advance matters by taking a gun to shatter the gate but Allen saw through his glass that it was built up with mud and correctly concluded that the attempt would fail.

Meanwhile, the army received some of its own medicine from a devastating barrage of Afghan guns fired from the surrounding hills: 'I fancy that very few who were there had ever been under the fire of round shot before. None but those who have experienced it can conceive how immense is the difference between watching the practice of your own guns against the enemy, and that of the enemy against you!' (*Diary*, 248). A brisk fire-fight ensued, Allen remarking on the high spirits and jocularity of the British soldiers as they were in the thick of the action. An Irish sergeant had his head grazed by a ball and confused he cried: '"Och! Somebody take my piece! I'm kilt-I'm kilt- I'm kilt". As they were leading him off, he looked over his shoulder, and cried out, "Faith boys, and I don't think I'm kilt *entirely* yet!" His second thought called forth shouts of laughter' (*Diary*, 250–1).

Allen himself had a close shave when he was helping to get a wounded officer into a litter (*doolie*) and staunching his blood. His groom noticed that a group of horsemen was approaching them from the fort as the delay caused by attending to the wounded man and finding a litter had caused Allen to be separated from the regiment. He urged the litter bearers to be off quickly and they managed to catch up without mishap and the group of Afghans withdrew.

As the British advanced the Afghans retreated leaving the field to the invaders. Allen estimated that the numbers of the enemy had been about 7,000 of whom around 50 were killed in the fight to capture their guns. These and their ammunition were British and came from Ghazni: some of those who had fired them were sepoys who had deserted on its surrender, including a drummer whose body was found amongst the dead. Only one British soldier was killed throughout the action, with twenty-seven wounded, an astonishingly low total. Allen did not count the camp followers, however, although he recorded that two lost legs during the fire-fight. We know that the Afghans could take deadly aim with their rifles so it must be supposed that they shot at too great a distance or while on the move (*jezails* were most effective when fired from rests). They possibly assumed that the sepoy deserters from Ghazni had a greater degree of expertise with their heavy guns than they actually possessed: the presence of a drummer amongst the artillery men bears this out. The British took two guns and a great deal of ammunition that the enemy had captured at the fall of Ghazni. After a hearty dinner with the 40th Allen retired to his tent to give thanks in prayer for the satisfactory outcome of the battle of Goyain.

The following day the fort of Goyain and several surrounding it were found to be abandoned. Inside many articles looted at Ghazni were discovered: officers' boots with brass spurs, camp bedsteads, swords etc. as well as useful supplies such as grain, fodder and wood from the doors and roofs. The forts were then burned with the enthusiastic assistance of the Hazaras, they were the enemies of the Sunni Ghilzais who had used the forts to oppress them. The Hazaras themselves had many forts in the area and Allen learnt that they were Shias who were from a different race to the Ghilzais and spoke Persian: their faces were round and flat so they resembled Tartars (see Part I, Chapter 6). The two peoples had been enemies for many generations and regularly shot at each other from their forts. Only the women, who were respected, could venture out to farm and collect food.

During an interview with General Nott the Hazara chieftains wished to impress three things on his mind:

1, That every Soonee was a wretch, whose throat they trusted he would cut without mercy; 2, that every man speaking the Affghan tongue was a villain, who should share the same fate; 3, that they hoped he would level the walls of Ghuznee, which were a serious inconvenience to them. We smiled at these merciful suggestions, but, with regard to Ghuznee, the general assured them of his willingness not only to destroy the defences, but to blow up the huge sixty-eight pounder gun, Zubber Jung [the mighty in battle], which they appeared to hold in great awe.

(Diary, 260)

On 2 September the army marched 9 miles to Oosa Kaureez where Allen was distressed by the sale in camp of the effects of Captains Bury and Reeves. This was normal practice whilst on campaign to enable the living to benefit from the useful objects left behind by the dead. He thought with dismay of the probable slaughter of more comrades at Ghazni and prayed that such a calamity should be averted. On 3 September, whilst they were on their way to Nanee, his apprehensions were increased when they realised that they were being tailed by about 150 Afghan horsemen. They kept out of range and had evidently been sent from Ghazni to report on the condition of the army as it approached.

At the same time that General Nott's army was making its way from Kandahar to Ghazni, General Pollock, accompanied by General Sale, had commenced his shorter march from Jalalabad to Kabul, a distance of about 100 miles. When he heard that, at last, they were to advance Sale wrote to him: 'Hurrah! This is good news. All here are prepared to meet your wishes to march as light as possible. I take no carriage from the Commissariat, and our officers are doubling up four in a small hill tent . . . I am so excited that I can scarce write' (Macrory, 258). They left Jalalabad on 20 August and had the unpleasant experience of following in reverse the route taken by Elphinstone's doomed force in January: from Gandamak to Boothak it was covered in their corpses in various stages of decay.

Pollock's force was larger, better fed and armed than their predecessors and the weather was warm but they still had hard fighting to get through the passes. This led Lieutenant Joseph Greenwood, HM 31st Regiment of

Foot, to compare the strengths of their enemy with those of the British soldiers:

> Our men were continually struck with the Affghan bullets, when we could reach the enemy with nothing under a six-pounder. Our muskets were useless when playing at long bowls. The fact is, our muskets are about as bad specimens of fire-arms as can be manufactured. The triggers are so stiff, that pulling them completely destroys any aim the soldier may take; and, when the machine goes off, the recoil is almost enough to knock a man backwards. Again the ball so much smaller than the bore of the barrel that accuracy in its flight, at any considerable distance is impossible. The clumsy flintlocks, also, are constantly missing fire . . .There is no weapon like the bayonet in the hands of a British soldier. The Affghans would stand like statues against firing, but the sight of the bristling line of cold steel they could not endure.
>
> (Greenwood, 139–40, 148)

General Nott's army arrived at Ghazni on 4 September after a march of 8 miles. It lay on the spur of a chain of hills with an attractive plain before it dotted with villages, forts, fields and gardens (Illustration 15). Hills rose behind it and up in the village of Bullool they could see many people, mainly horsemen, but the town itself showed no signs of life and no flags were displayed. They camped near a walled garden; to their surprise they were not attacked and Allen's Sunday service at 5.00 pm was well attended. He urged: 'them to seek that reconciliation with God, through the blood of Christ, which affords the only well-grounded hope of a blessed immortality, from the great probability that some who were present might be destined never to attend another service' (*Diary*, 263–4). Their peace was ended during the night when some *ghazis* approached the garden and started firing into the camp. They were kept at bay but a few men were wounded and it was very hard to sleep.

The next day, 5 September, saw the battle for Ghazni that Allen had so much feared. The camp was moved to the east of the town to assist the start of operations and to avoid, they thought, the attentions of the awful Zubber

Jung and the 16th NI went out to reconnoitre the walls hoping to find a weak spot to breach. The Afghan horsemen from Bullool and the surrounding hills came down to attack and footmen with rifles remained up in the village to discomfort the British. Guns were sent forward and much of the army advanced including the 40th and 41st. Allen watched through his glass from a small garden where he had a good view. The light companies ascended the heights and in the face of heavy fire gradually pushed back the defenders who also vacated Bullool.

Believing that there was to be a lull in hostilities, Allen and some of the officers of the 40th were going to the mess tent for breakfast when they were deafened by a huge bang and whirring, their first acquaintance with Zubber Jung, fired from the citadel in Ghazni. The shot flew over the mess tent, wounded some camels, ricocheted over the mess tent of the 41st and killed a camel. No one wanted any breakfast after that and orders came to move the camp immediately to safety. It had been thought that the great gun could only be fired from a fixed position but this was soon disproved. One of the huge shots, more than 50lb of hammered iron, had been carried to Nott's tent and a large number of officers were inspecting it when, after a pause to bring it round, another shot was fired over the tent. Strangely (or by Providence as Allen would have it) no one was killed or wounded during the three hours that it took to move the camp, even when men and animals were huddled together, although four or five camels were lost. In the meantime a way of silencing the great gun had been devised: Lieutenant Terry took two nine-pounders up to the top of the Bullool hills and was able to fire down amongst the gunners who served Zubber Jung and no more was heard from it. The army spent a peaceful night and Allen slept soundly after he had repeated his earnest prayers that Ghazni would not be stormed.

The following day, 6 September, Allen awoke to find to his joy that the enemy had left Ghazni undefended. They had probably calculated that a breaching battery would be turned against them and, after their experience of the assault by General Keane in 1839, had no appetite for it. This reinforced Allen's view that whilst individual Afghan fighters could be brave and resourceful they were no match for a disciplined British force in the field. He followed Nott and a large party of officers into the town and first examined the walls concluding that, since in some places they were composed of rubble, stone and mud, they could fairly easily have been breached. He was disappointed at the appearance of Ghazni, 'mean, confined and dirty': many houses had been destroyed during the assaults by Keane in 1839 and the Afghans in early 1842. On the latter occasion when they took the town the *ghazis* murdered the Hindus, the wealthiest portion of the population, and destroyed their houses.

Allen inspected Zubber Jung, which was made of brass, on its clumsy carriage beneath the citadel and regretted that it could not be taken back to India. Behind were rooms used by the British as barracks during their occupation of Ghazni, 1839 to 1842, and then as the officers' prison. Several names and sentences were scratched on the walls and a message from Lieutenant Harris of the 27th NI which Allen copied and gave to Major Leech. It recorded the bad treatment that they had all suffered from their captors especially the commander, Colonel Palmer, who had been tortured. The copies of the treaties he had made with the local leaders, who had subsequently reneged on them, were found concealed in a beam of the room. Apart from examining the town for evidence concerning their predecessors, the soldiers were able to take away good stocks of grain, fodder and wood.

In the evening Allen accompanied a large party of officers to visit the tomb of Mahmood of Ghazni, it was made of alabaster and situated in a rather mean building surrounded by a garden. Allen was especially disappointed by the decayed state of the celebrated sandalwood gates that the conquering Mahmood was said to have looted from the Hindu temple of Shiva in Somnath, Gujarat, India in the eleventh century. To the dismay of the local holy men, they were dismantled by the engineers together with the doorposts and lintel and put in the keeping of the 40th but they were careful, Allen stressed, to do no other damage to the revered tomb. Lord Ellenborough believed that the restoration of the gates to India would be a great propaganda coup, although they were eventually given a rather cool reception. Muslims were furious at their loss as were the Sikhs who had hoped to get them as a reward for their (not very effective) support of the British.

During the halt at Ghazni 327 sepoys of the 27th NI arrived in camp, they had been sold into slavery, but when Ghazni was re-taken by the British their masters fled from the town and surrounding villages so they escaped. Nott had a high opinion of sepoys, he wrote of their behaviour at Ghazni: 'some sharp skirmishing, in which our sepoys behaved to admiration' (Stocqueler, vol. 2, 262). Yet Nott has been contrasted unfavourably with Pollock for not taking maimed sepoys and camp followers who had escaped back to India. The fate of such sepoys and camp followers is harder to trace than that of Europeans since contemporary commentators were often less interested in them.

On 9 September the camp was moved to Roseh 2 miles in the direction of Kabul to shorten the march. The citadel of Ghazni was blown up as were some of the bastions of the outer walls, the gates were burnt and the guns, including Zubber Jung, were all burst. These operations to destroy a strong fortress must have sent a clear message to the Afghans that the British no longer intended to stay in their country. Allen indignantly refuted later reports that orchards and fruit trees were destroyed by the army. He pointed out that they had enough to do in breaking down the town's defences before their departure: although when such a large body of people, soldiers, followers and beasts passed through the country some damage was bound to occur. The army certainly benefited from the abundance of the valley, enjoying apples, pears, plums, grapes, water melons, cabbages, carrots, beetroot and other produce. Fortified by all this plenty and rejoicing in delightful weather the army re-commenced its march to Kabul.

CHAPTER 5

Kabul, 'The Bazaars were Very Handsome for Affghanistan'

The converging armies of Generals Pollock and Nott had some hard fighting to do before they reached Kabul but, once there, opposition melted away. The British dilemma was to make a proportionate response to what they viewed as the Afghan duplicity that had led to the destruction of General Elphinstone's army. An expedition to punish Kohistan and the destruction of the Great Bazaar might have been justifiable measures: the undisciplined looting that followed was not.

Ghazni had proved difficult to take in the recent past: both General Keane in 1838 and the besieging Afghans in early 1842 had fought hard for it. General Nott could congratulate himself in September that good discipline, high morale, adequate supplies and the terror that his name inspired had delivered this strategic town into his hands with very small losses. He had little else to be pleased about however: until the Kabul disaster he had expected to become commander there once Elphinstone had left for India. Instead, he and his men had endured a hard and embattled winter in Kandahar with little food and without any help from India until General England arrived in early May. By that time the garrison through their own exertions had improved the flow of supplies and won several victories over their enemies. General Pollock was to be appointed supreme commander over all the forces in Afghanistan and Nott's reaction has been compared to Achilles sulking in his tent during the Trojan War.

Nott's army left Ghazni on 10 September and marched for 10½ miles to Shushgao. It was getting very cold during the nights, an ominous sign that they could not afford to stay in Afghanistan for too long. The following day was a Sunday so after the march Allen held his usual service at 5.00 pm. During the night the camp was fired on although no one was hurt, the pickets responded and three of the enemy were killed. The worst thing about these night attacks was that it deprived the exhausted army of its sleep; Allen seems to have been affected particularly badly.

Everyone had an uncomfortable day on 12 September: they camped at Sidabad, a site that was shut in by ravines and ditches and provided excellent cover for their enemies. The area had an evil reputation since at the beginning of the revolt, on 3 November 1841, Captain Woodburn, 44th Bengal Regiment Native Infantry and 150 sepoys were massacred there. He had been promised protection in a yard beside the fort but the Afghans immediately began to fire down on him from its walls: he tried to escape but was shot down with his men. Nott's force found the fort was abandoned but some of Woodburn's possessions, including a complimentary letter from Sir William Macnaghten, were still lying around there. The fort and another one nearby were blown up and then burnt. The continuing danger was brought home to the force by the murder of two privates who had foolishly strolled unarmed by the Kabul river; a group of the enemy found them and cut them to pieces and Allen buried the remains. Throughout the night his sleep was again disturbed by small-fire from the ravines and hollows accompanied by blood-curdling shrieks and yells. One sentry was killed and another died of his wounds a few days later.

The following day the army had a difficult march of 7 miles since the road was narrow and bad along the crumbling and precipitous banks of the Loghur river. At Shakabad the force had to cross a long narrow bridge and, half way, Allen realised that it was full of holes and very dangerous. He could not turn back because of the press of men and animals behind him so he dismounted intending to lead his horse. At that moment it slipped, knocked Allen down onto the bridge and fell into the river. Fortunately, it was near enough the bank to scramble out unscathed but he realised that if he had still been on its back when it fell he would probably have been killed. Another sleepless night passed due to the continual gunfire. It was enlivened, however, by the arrival of a Kuzzilbashi chief with twenty-five horse who had deserted Akbar Khan: a good sign since they were well known for backing the winners in any conflict.

On 14 September Nott's force marched across a plain to Beni-badam, 3 miles short of Maidan where they thought that Shumshoodeen Khan would launch another attack. Before making their camp they took the heights of a small pass that led to Maidan, suffering two dead and several wounded in the process. This turned out to have been a futile action, caused by a misunderstanding with the quarter-master, as the camp was on the southern side of the pass and, as soon as the light companies withdrew, the enemy re-occupied it. One of those who had been killed was the bugler of the 40th, a very popular long-serving man who was greatly mourned by the regiment. The Afghans started firing from the re-occupied heights leading to the pass and everyone expected another disturbed night. They were too far away to do much damage but, after a ball fell amongst his camels, Allen got his terrified servants to make a screen from his luggage to protect themselves. Before they went to bed an eighteen-pounder full of grapeshot was fired at the enemy with a huge noise and after that everything went quiet and Allen enjoyed his first good sleep for some time. Nott received a letter from Pollock announcing that he had defeated Akbar Khan at Tezeen and would enter Kabul on 14 or 15 September.

Nott marched on Maidan through the pass the following day keeping to the right side of the road and flanked by the horse artillery that fired continuously up into the hills, so his men and the baggage the Afghans wanted to steal were unscathed. Allen was amazed at the effrontery of a well-dressed Afghan who rode up to Major Leech on a fine horse and asked for a paper to give his villages protection from the army. As he admitted that he had been fighting them the day before, it was hardly surprising that the general sent him off with a flea in his ear, 'I thought he got off very easily'.

As Allen ascended to the top of the pass:

One of the most impressive scenes I have ever beheld burst upon me. On one side of the ridge was the imposing military cavalcade crowding the valley I had left; the artillery vomiting forth smoke and fire; thousands of bayonets glittering in the sun; cavalry, regular and

137

irregular, in their variegated uniforms; horses prancing and neighing; bugles sounding; everything life and animation; the whole closed by a dark brown mass of many thousand camels, slowly emerging from clouds of dust. On the other side was a most exquisite green valley, deeply imbedded in lofty purple mountains, watered by a clear gushing river, dotted over with fortified villages amidst topes [groves] of poplars, and surrounded by green fields of maize, rice, vetches, and wheat.

(*Diary*, 290–1)

As he watched this peaceful scene the native soldiery crowned the heights and, in the course of a few hours, the crops had been taken and the camp followers had ransacked and burnt the villages, the 'prosperity of years was desolated in less than a day'.

Despite the overwhelming force employed by the British there was still some hard fighting to do at Maidan. Allen thought that he was well out of range of the snipers until a ball buried itself in the ground at his feet and another passed through the forage cap of a captain of the 40th. The rearguard had a very sharp skirmish since the Afghans came down into the plain with unusual confidence because the axel-tree of one of the nine-pounders had broken. The redoubtable Lieutenant Terry, however, turned his remaining gun on them and killed about fifty. The army reached Maidan with few casualties and heard the good news that General Pollock had taken Kabul and was in possession of the Bala Hissar. Captain Troup, Captain and Mrs Anderson and their children, Dr Campbell and Mrs Trevor and her children had been rescued. Apart from Captain Troup, who had been in almost perpetual motion on behalf of the prisoners, Akbar Khan and the generals at Jalalabad, the others had been so sick that they had remained at Shewaki when the rest of the captives were hurried off to Bamian.

Nott's army marched 9 miles to Urghundee on 16 September and camped on some rather damp ground. They were, however, surrounded by attractive gardens and the friendly locals brought them ample supplies. In the course of the day they heard that the dashing Sir Richmond Shakespear was riding towards Bamian with 600 Kuzzilbashis to look for the main group of prisoners. The next day Nott marched to within 5 miles of Kabul and camped on the west side of a gorge leading to the valley in which the city stood. They could see part of the Bala Hissar and were relaxed enough to enjoy the temperate climate and gardens full of delicious fruit.

The 18 September was a Sunday and Allen was gratified by the good attendance at his evening service. He had spent a tranquil day meditating on the mercy of God and praying for the safe return of the prisoners. General Pollock paid General Nott a visit and exercised his considerable charm and tact since he realised that Nott would be feeling resentful that he was, now that the armies had merged, only second in command in Afghanistan. Later in the day the good news arrived that Shakespear had found the prisoners, they were all safe but he feared that the Afghans would attempt to re-capture them and asked Pollock to send a brigade to assist him. Possibly thinking that he would flatter the thin-skinned general, he ordered Nott to send a force.

Nott wrote to Pollock:

> My Dear General you express a wish that I should detach a brigade towards Bamian. Before you decide on sending it I would beg to state as follows: 1st The troops under my command have just made a long and very difficult march of upwards of thirty miles, and they have been continually marching about for the last six months, and most certainly require rest for a day or two, the same with my camels and other cattle. I lost twenty-nine camels yesterday, and expect today's report will be double that number. 2nd I am getting short of supplies, and can see but little probability of getting a quantity equal to my daily consumption at this place. I have little or no money. 3rd I have so many sick and wounded that I fear I shall have the greatest inconvenience and difficulty in carrying them . . . 4th I sincerely think that sending a small detachment will and must be followed by deep disaster. No doubt Mahomed Acbur Shumshoodeen and the other Chiefs are uniting their forces, and I hourly expect to hear that Sir R. Shakespear is added to the number of British prisoners.

(Stocqueler, vol. 2, 142–3)

He concluded by saying that he would, nevertheless, obey the order if Pollock wished and regretted that he had to write a response since ill-health prevented him from delivering his message in person. Allen voiced the feelings of many of Nott's officers when he wrote that he was sorry that they had lost the honour of escorting the prisoners.

Was Nott simply sulking? Mackenzie reported his view that he did not see why he should risk his men when the British government had not lifted a finger to rescue the prisoners for months (and he knew all too well how close Ellenborough had been to leaving Afghanistan without attempting to save them). 'Fighting Bob' Sale had already been in Kabul for several days and his men had marched less than half the distance from Jalalabad that Nott's men had covered in their journey from Kandahar. Sale was asked to take a brigade instead and accepted the task with alacrity: they passed Allen's camp on their way early the next morning.

On the evening of 20 September Allen was returning from holding a service at the military hospital when he saw a little crowd of officers surrounding one of the Ghazni captives who had just come in: others had gone to Pollock's camp. He was Captain Alston, 27th NI, who was wearing native dress and looking healthy and 'very like an Afghan'; he was nearly overwhelmed by the press of people and their questions. Allen later saw Major Eldred Pottinger and gave his opinion that he had been largely responsible through his exertions for the prisoners at Bamian in gaining their freedom several days before Shakespear arrived. By the evening Allen was able to count 117 prisoners and hostages from Kabul, Bamian and Ghazni who had been liberated.

Nott's army moved 3 miles nearer to the city on 21 September, not far from the pleasant site of Emperor Babur's tomb (see Part I, Chapter 1). Just as Allen was getting his tent pitched he met Captain Walsh, 52nd Madras Regiment Native Infantry, who had been one of the hostages surrendered to Akbar Khan before the British departure from Kabul in early January. He stayed and talked for nearly an hour, Allen noted the good quality of the Afghan dress that he was wearing and was told that they had been well treated by Akbar. After breakfast Major Hibbert of the 40th made up a party to visit Kabul, which the ever curious Allen eagerly joined.

The group of officers rode through narrow, half-ruinous and deserted streets to the Bala Hissar. Its lower area was part of the city, as distinct from the palace, which they entered near the bastion that Akbar had blown up and passed through a little bazaar where fruit and grain were for sale. In a square Allen counted twenty-eight guns, some British the rest Afghan, and later saw three others, relics of the recent occupation by Shah Shujah's son, Futteh Jung, and subsequently by Akbar. The officers then entered the palace enclosure but could not go into the royal residence because Futteh Jung had re-possessed it, 'keeping up a shadow of sovereignty'. Allen regretted the terrible state of the gardens which he thought would once have been very beautiful but appreciated the great hall where *durbars* were held with its fine, painted ceilings, cornices and richly carved lattices. They then climbed to the citadel, at the highest point of the Bala Hissar, where the British flag was flying and enjoyed the magnificent view including the old *cantonments* (Illustration 16): 'It was melancholy indeed to stand and gaze on the very spot which had witnessed the humiliation and disgrace of our arms, and the destruction of such multitudes' (*Diary*, 302). He estimated that Kabul was more than twice the size of Kandahar and that the Bala Hissar occupied about a quarter of it.

The party then rode through the Great Bazaar, 'very handsome for Affghanistan'; the shops had roofs covered in carved woodwork and with arched fronts. At intervals there were basins for water but nothing had flowed into them for a long time. They later came to a ruined mosque and inside visited the tomb of Shah Shujah that lay in a small dark room. His body, the *fakirs* informed them, was buried beneath a thin layer of earth forming a mound. It was covered with a mat and, finally, a kind of counterpane on which he had been reclining in his palanquin when he was murdered: it was white but covered with black blood stains, 'a remarkable lesson on the unsatisfactory nature of the pursuits of human ambition'.

Returning through the city they met General Sale's brigade coming in with the prisoners on the last stage of their journey from Bamian. The ladies were in litters (there was no mention of whether or not Lady Sale was riding on a horse), the gentlemen were in litters (some were still sick) or on horseback and the troops were either on foot or riding on camels. They were accompanied by a number of elephants that were used for carriage and Allen was surprised by their speed and agility. Despite this cheerful sight, they were depressed to pass the ruined house of Sir Alexander Burnes which was peppered with scars from musket balls.

During the evening one of the liberated Ghazni officers, Lieutenant Nicholson, 27th NI, dined at the mess where he had become an honorary member. He was very young and was admired for the bravery with which he had defended the Water Gate at Ghazni. He confirmed that the prisoners had been harshly treated by Shumshoodeen Khan but that things had greatly improved once they were transferred to Akbar Khan. When they first arrived he invited them to dinner and showed them great hospitality and kindness. Allen could think of no other instance, even in European warfare, of a prince entertaining 'his prisoners of inferior rank at his own table!'.

A party of officers made an excursion to the tomb of the Emperor Babur on 23 September. They crossed an ancient stone bridge over the Kabul river on which another group of officers were fishing. The weather was delightful and the scenery, when they entered the tomb enclosure, resembled an English park, clear water cascaded down a series of terraces and near the top there was a fine white marble mosque that bore the date '1640' (Illustration 17). Beyond it were the tombs of the emperor and his daughter, the latter surrounded by an exquisite marble screen of flowered open-work. The contrast between these peaceful and harmless pursuits and the horrors the British army had experienced in Kabul less than a year previously could not have been greater.

On the following day Allen rode through Kabul to Pollock's camp taking a route that led him past the Kuzzilbashi quarter. He was glad to see that it was surrounded by a strong wall and well guarded at the gate, since he had heard that the city was to be burnt and he hoped that the lives and property of these people who had, on the whole, been pro-British would be spared. When he arrived at the camp he called on several of the ladies and baptised three infants who had been born in captivity, he did not name them so we do not know whether or not they included Alexandrina Sturt's little girl. He was fascinated to hear about:

> all they had been compelled to endure, from the severity of the weather, rapid travelling, etc., though they seemed to have

experienced all the alleviations of which such a situation was capable, and the character of Ackbar Khan rose the higher the more one heard of him. He appears to be in humanity and courtesy far in advance of the generality of his countrymen. Both the ladies and the children looked remarkably healthy.

(*Diary*, 309)

Lady Sale had finished her *Journal* by that time but here, and in his other meetings with the prisoners, Allen's experience of the war converged with hers.

On Sunday 25 September Allen held a service for the European troops at sunrise, the text of his sermon, was Deuteronomy, iv, 39–40 and it was a reflection on the whole course of the war since the original invasion nearly four years previously. His text enjoined the Israelites to keep God's commandments if they wished to prosper. Arrogance and ungodly behaviour had beset the British army and they had been terribly punished but heavenly grace had allowed small bands to survive, combine with the relieving force which 'now stands victorious almost in view of the site of that most awful catastrophe'. Much of this was achieved by the officers and men but they should not forget that it was finally due to Providence and should live their lives in future as good Christians. He preached to the officers on another text in the evening.

On the next day they saw snow on the hills for the first time: an ominous sign that the army should soon be on its way back to India if it was to escape another catastrophe. Before it left, however, it had to demonstrate British power and punish at least some of those who had humiliated it. The town of Istalif in Kohistan had been one of the first places to defy the government of Shah Shujah so it was an obvious target for retribution. General McCaskill and Brigadier Stacey were dispatched with two brigades and news arrived a few days later that they had taken it and Charikar (where the British garrison had been destroyed the previous November) at the cost of the death of one lieutenant: Allen did not mention casualties amongst other ranks on this occasion. The two towns were burnt and many Afghans were killed but Allen indignantly refuted, as he had done at Ghazni, press allegations that atrocities were perpetrated on the population and their orchards. He had made careful enquiries and was convinced that the general standard of conduct was good, assisted no doubt by the absence of liquor in the towns to fuel the appetites of the conquerors. It was a matter of common sense that Kohistan was about 40 miles in extent, covered in orchards, so two small brigades on a campaign of a mere ten days could not have done much damage. On the other hand, Lieutenant Greenwood mentioned a punitive expedition he joined in the summer from Jalalabad before the whole force marched on Kabul. He was sent as part of a brigade to Pesh Bolak to destroy the forts and villages of recalcitrant tribes and to kill their mulberry trees by cutting rings round their trunks.

For a few days Nott's army was occupied in moving camp to Shere Sung on the south side of the Jalalabad road, the route by which they would leave the country. On 1 October, in the company of an officer, Allen visited a community of thirty-five Armenian Christians in Kabul, composed of four families of men, women and children. The Reverend Piggott had discovered them and baptised two of their children when he accompanied General Keane as chaplain to 'the army of the Indus' in 1839 and told his friend Allen about them. They had a property up a narrow alley in the Bala Hissar and all lived round a small courtyard that also contained a church. Allen described the lovingly kept interior in detail, including its furniture and holy books. They lived by making Shiraz wine and spirits but were persecuted by the Afghans who extorted heavy sums from them. Allen was not sure whether or not they were as poor as they seemed but he was convinced that they were respectable: displays of wealth would in any case have been unwise. It could be that they enjoyed some protection from the chiefs in Kabul by living in the Bala Hissar. Allen's evidence about the Kuzzilbashi chief shows that not all Muslims took the prohibition of wine entirely seriously. The Armenians welcomed him warmly as they had not been visited by one of their own priests for thirteen years.

On the next day, a Sunday, Allen went to Pollock's camp to hold a service for a large number of soldiers. Generals Pollock and Sale and many of the officers who had been prisoners were present. At the end about forty men of the 13th (Sale's regiment) gave Allen great pleasure by singing Psalm cvi beautifully with a large number of the congregation joining in,

'O render thanks to God above'. 'It was many, many months since I had heard a psalm from any other voice than my own, and this was refreshing indeed' (*Diary*, 314–15).

There was plenty of scope for Allen to work as a priest in Kabul with an army, the released prisoners and the Armenians to care for. He visited the latter small community again in the company of several officers who were fascinated by their church and its contents: the Armenians allowed them to examine everything provided they left their swords outside. Allen baptised three infants by immersion in a large vessel of lukewarm water; afterwards he and his companions were entertained with tea and cakes in an upper room. He saw the two pretty children who had been baptised by the Reverend Pigott three years previously. When he had asked the Armenians why they remained in Afghanistan where they were treated so harshly, they had replied, 'How can we leave our church?' Allen said 'goodbye' and left sadly knowing that he was unlikely ever to meet them again and hoping that the religion they shared would one day prosper in the hostile country of Afghanistan.

During the night of 8 October Allen was summoned to General Pollock's camp to minister to Lieutenant Scott of the 13th, who was seriously ill with an abscess on his liver. He was very weak but calm and they discussed his preparation for receiving Holy Communion and prayed together; Allen spent the rest of the night in an adjoining tent. Scott seemed a little better the following morning, a Sunday, so Allen rode back to Nott's camp to hold a service. He returned quickly to Pollock's camp, as Scott's condition had deteriorated, gave him communion and witnessed his will which seemed to comfort him. Allen remarked on the kindness and solicitude of the sick man's fellow officers:

> Those who see a soldier in the glitter of gay society at home, have little conception of what he really is. It is in the field, in the absence of almost every comfort, in the face of disease and death, that his real character is developed, and exhibits, often in mere boys, a tenderness of heart, a delicacy of attention, and extent of self-denial, that would astonish and perhaps shame many of their seniors who are more

happily situated.

(Diary, 320)

In the afternoon Allen held a service attended by many of the recently liberated ladies (probably out of politeness, he never mentioned them by name). His text was Psalm cvii, 1–2. 'Let them give thanks whom the Lord hath redeemed and delivered from the hand of the enemy.' He outlined the sufferings they had endured: their experience of a false, cruel religion and the probability that they might have remained in captivity. Their release was providential and they should show their gratitude by being, as if newborn, living good Christian lives and dedicating their children to God's service. If Lady Sale was in the congregation one wonders how she reacted. Allen spent the evening with Scott and slept at Pollock's camp: the officer presumably died before they left Kabul but he did not mention him again.

Allen was greatly distressed on 10 and 11 October by the destruction of the central building of the Great Bazaar and the plunder that ensued by European soldiers, sepoys and camp followers there and in other parts of Kabul. As the former was the site of the terrible scene when the mangled body of Sir William Macnaghten was displayed it was perhaps an inevitable consequence, but neither Pollock nor Nott seem to have done anything to stop the sequel:

> every kind of disgraceful outrage was suffered to go on in the town. The shops were broken open and rifled; every sort of plunder was displayed and offered for sale in the lines of both camps, which were like a fair; and an utter disorganisation of the force appeared likely to ensue if this state of things were to continue; and this after a quiet halt of more than twenty days, when we had replenished the commissariat supplies by the assistance of these poor people, who had returned to their shops upon an express proclamation of protection in the event of their doing so!

(Diary, 321)

Allen's decent reaction to the destruction may not have been typical of opinion in the army. Lieutenant Robert Carey belonged to the 40th, although Allen mentioned him only in passing and they were unlikely to have been soul mates. Writing to his father on 7 October 1842, after criticising Pollock for trying to conciliate the Afghans, he observed: 'Cabool is a beautiful place and I hope to see its beauty spoilt before we leave it . . . Now we have all the prisoners and all the guns we may leave the country with more honour than any of us ever expected' (Army Museum Library, 5912-146, typescript). Generals Pollock and Nott had usually enforced high standards of discipline throughout their campaigns, although they probably felt that, with some tough marching and fighting ahead, the soldiers could be allowed some licence before they quitted Kabul, but it left a baleful heritage. The result of these outrages was a terrible memory of the British, who usually prided themselves on occupying the moral high ground. They had kept some friends in Afghanistan throughout the war: pro-Western chiefs, Hindus and Kuzzilbashis and some of these would have been afflicted by the ravages of the army. As Kaye remarked of the war in general: 'The Afghans are an unforgiving race; and everywhere, from Candahar to Caubul, and from Caubul to Peshawur, were traces of the injuries we had inflicted upon the tribes' (Kaye, vol. 3, 399).

It only remained to 'settle' the government of Kabul before the army left for the arduous march to Ferozepore in India: Futteh Jung prudently decided to leave with the British. His younger brother, Shahpoor, was left in the Bala Hissar with four six-pounders belonging to the East India Company: no one was optimistic about his chances of survival. Allen had inspected the old *cantonments* and, having read part of Captain Johnson's journals, he concluded: 'if those in command had displayed from the first that moderate degree of presence of mind and energy which might reasonably have been expected from them, neither the force of the enemy, nor the rigour of the season, could, humanly speaking, have produced such disastrous effects' (*Diary*, 323).

CHAPTER 6

'Ladies Upon Enormous Elephants', the Return to Ferozepore

As the British army left Afghanistan via Jalalabad and the Khyber pass they were incessantly harried by the tribes who had not been bribed to allow them a peaceful journey and wished to show their hatred of the infidel feringhees. A pleasant journey through the Punjab culminated in a huge reception given by the Governor General, Lord Ellenborough, at Ferozepore. The festivities were pretentious and slightly ridiculous but Allen felt that, despite criticism in the press, British honour had been restored by the excellent work of the army.

Allen had started on his journey from Bombay as a *griffin* in May 1841, a year and a half before General Pollock's army quit Kabul. He had covered a huge area and suffered losses of property, extremes of weather, the dangers of battle and, worst of all, the death of comrades, most of whom he then buried. Throughout he had remained positive and enthusiastic about new sights and experiences, even when he was critical of the British government and the Afghans. The last phase of the campaign, the march from Kabul, via Jalalabad to Ferozepore where the army disbanded, proved an altogether darker experience for the clergyman who was by then a seasoned campaigner. He still appreciated the beauties of the landscape and the camaraderie of the soldiers but there were reasons for a change in his mood apart from the fact that the charm of novelty had worn off. Allen and the rest of the army were afflicted by the awful scenes of death and decay as they retraced the rout of the fatal retreat of Elphinstone's force. Lady Sale and the other prisoners had already suffered a similar experience but

Pollock's army was obliged several times to camp in the middle of the carnage. The knowledge that they would have to march through the most dangerous and difficult of all the passes, the Khyber, added to the force's feelings of depression and foreboding.

Pollock led his division of the army out of their camp at Kabul on the morning of 12 October and Nott's force followed: the two were meant to remain apart but Nott soon caught up with Pollock's rear-guard and chaos ensued. The camels were mixed together, especially as they all tried to cross a river by a small bridge when their loads kept falling off. On the way they got an intimation of what was to come as the road was lined with the corpses of sepoys and camp followers from the January retreat, Allen counted seventy. On the first day of the retreat they had been killed not so much by Afghans but by the extreme cold and the near starvation they had suffered before their departure. It took Pollock and Nott six hours to march 8 miles and when they arrived near Boothak, to Allen's disgust, there was no mess tent so no dinner! His baggage did at least arrive and he shared his tent with an officer who was not so fortunate. The army remained at Boothak for the following day, on the very spot where Elphinstone had camped in January, it was a most uncongenial place to stop. Apart from the bodies, all sorts of reminders of the dead were lying around: fragments of clothing, combs, gloves and broken china. Allen did not give the reason for the delay but they may have wished to reorganise their cavalcade to avoid further confusion. The weather was benign, reaching 74 degrees in the shade in the afternoon.

The next day, 14 October, was a terrible one for Allen and the army since they had to march through the Khoord Kabul pass, the narrow defile and overhanging rocks of which made the heights almost impossible to crown if they were opposed. Allen understood how difficult it must have been for Elphinstone's starved, freezing and demoralised army to pass this obstacle and around him were many of those who had not made it. In the grey morning light with carrion crows and vultures flapping overhead he saw many bodies, for example:

in one place twelve skeletons, huddled together in a little nook. Some, from their attitudes, appeared to be those of persons who had expired in great agony, probably from wounds. Most of them retained their hair, and the skin had dried on the bones, so the hands and feet were little altered in form. Some were still covered with fragments of clothing, and here and there the uniform was discoverable. The horse and his rider lay side by side, or men were seen clasped in each other's arms, as they had crowded together for the warmth. One spot, where the path was almost closed by rocks projecting from either side, was literally choked with the corpses of men, horses and camels. It appeared as if a tremendous volley had been poured among them, or that the delay unavoidable in passing so narrow a gorge had caused them to drop from cold.

(*Diary*, 328–9)

The force passed through 5 miles of the Khoord Kabul unscathed but they encountered the body of a Brahmin who appeared to have been murdered during the previous night, a warning that hostile eyes were watching them. Even when they emerged from the pass and camped for the remainder of the day they were oppressed by the awful sights they had seen.

The following day was equally trying: a march of 14 miles over 'as bad a road as can well be conceived'. Heaps of bodies lay in hideous attitudes and more were huddled in roadside caves. At the Huft Kotul (eight hills) horses, baggage animals and guns had to negotiate eight successive sudden dips in the road. They counted fifty-seven dead and dying camels and eight horses from General Pollock's march on the previous day, and worse was to come. They saw the bodies of a *naick* (native corporal), five sepoys, a messenger, two camel-men and an old female Hindu camp follower, most of them badly mangled, from Pollock's force. The fact that even the sepoys had been left behind indicated to Allen that the army had been hard pressed. As they arrived at their camp at Tezeen they heard firing and saw that General McCaskill's rear-guard was exchanging shots with small parties of Afghans on the heights who were hoping to rush down and plunder the baggage. Pickets climbed up and dispersed them and Nott's baggage arrived unscathed, but they remained anxious about the fate of their rear-guard.

The 16 October was a Sunday but a very unsatisfactory one for Allen: he discovered that parts of the 40th and the 41st, led by Major Hibbert, had returned to the Huft Kotul during the previous night as he slept to assist Captain Leeson's rear-guard that was under heavy fire. They managed to gain command of several hills, dispersed the enemy and recovered their dead and wounded, the former including McCaskill's men from the previous day. Altogether ten Europeans and sepoys were killed and forty-two were wounded. The day's march of 7 miles to Seh Baba was bedevilled by the torrent that flowed down the road and caused havoc amongst the horses and camels. On the other hand, it had washed away most of the bodies left from the January retreat, apart from about 200 in a small tower near the camp. The enemy fired down at them but were too far away to do much damage: indeed when Allen celebrated a service for the officers in their mess tent in the afternoon, they observed smoke from the rifles through the open flaps with tranquillity.

The marches through such difficult terrain were taking their toll on the camels; on 17 October Allen estimated that Pollock and Nott both lost about 100 and this may have been why they progressed only for 5 miles to Kutty Sung. On the way Allen saw the pitiful sight of a little black dog guarding the body of its master (presumably a camp follower) that it would not allow anyone to approach. At camp they received the pleasing news that the Governor General was to award a medal to all the troops and six months *batta* (extra pay). Allen gave a graphic account of camp life in such wild and picturesque surroundings:

Towering hills, of various forms and distances, surround it on every side. On the ridge of each is seen, by day, a bristling line of piled arms of the out-lying-picket, the men sitting in groups or strolling along the ridge of the hills; as the sun declines, the same hills are occupied with lines of sentries, relieved against the horizon; after dark, little bright fires light up all around, and down in the hollows the voice of mirth and laughter is loud and general, till at last all sinks into silence, and the sound of the gongs striking the hour, the occasional challenge of a sentry, or the change of guard, are the only sounds that meet the ear, except for those universal nuisances of the camp, the bray of asses and the bark of *pariar* dogs. . . . All is still, if there be no alarm or attack, till the appointed hour, when a single bugle gives its shrill note from the adjutant-general's tent; the summons is taken up and repeated by bugles and drums from corps to corps; all spring into life and activity; tents are struck, camels are loaded, horses saddled, men fall in, and a very short time leaves the hills and the hollows as still and desolate as before.

(*Diary*, 337–8)

Allen had been obliged to burn a number of his possessions because of the difficulties his camels were experiencing with the terrain, for some had become very weak. They marched 7 miles to Jugdulluk on 18 October, a terrible place to spend the night with its association with the army's retreat in January. As they approached they could hear the fire of small arms and heavy guns as McCaskill's rear-guard was harassed from the heights. They saw the remains of about a hundred soldiers from the January retreat lying by some ruined walls, from the lightness of their skin, most seemed to be Europeans from the 44th and the horse artillery. One body lying by a horse they thought must have been an officer from the length of his hair, NCOs and privates were obliged to have their hair cut short. Allen remembered that it was from this place that General Elphinstone went to treat with Akbar Khan and was treacherously taken prisoner.

Before leaving Jugdulluk the next day the two remaining eighteen-pounders were blown up, General Nott had insisted on bringing them this far but the difficult terrain defeated even him. Two had already been destroyed at Khoord Kabul, necessary measures to relieve the bullocks, indeed men had been obliged to drag the guns most of the way through the passes. The march to Sourkab was 13 miles but it seemed longer to Allen who was feeling unwell: the sight of so much despair and death may have undermined his usually buoyant spirits and constitution. They were not attacked during the journey but, when they arrived at their camp, three sharpshooters were cheekily firing at the quarter-master's men as they erected the tents, although they were soon driven off. Major Simmonds's rear-guard was not so fortunate having 'very sharp work' losing several men and a lieutenant was seriously wounded.

On 20 October they reached Gandamack through much more open country, no one was hurt but they killed several Afghans. They were relieved to find plentiful supplies of fodder for the animals after dearth in the passes. Allen mused that he normally preferred mountain scenery to plains but here it was a relief to reach them since: 'to visit mountains in Wales or Switzerland is quite a different thing from passing through them bristling with *matchlocks*, and strewed with the dead bodies of one's fellow creatures and fellow countrymen' (*Diary*, 341). His satisfaction was increased by the arrival of a large packet of letters from India and England: like the rest of the army he had been cut off from communications with his homeland for several months. The next day the force rested after its arduous eight-day march through the passes, but one of Allen's camels disappeared and the camp was fired on.

A short march of 5 miles sufficed on 22 October. Allen admired the beauty of the now distant hills and presented an officer, who collected birds, with a pretty little partridge that one of his servants had caught. Soldiers' cultural and scientific interests in the eighteenth and nineteenth centuries are sometimes overlooked: there were artists in the army such as Eyre, Rattray and Atkinson, as well as botanists and, in this case, an ornithologist. The next day was a Sunday but when they camped at Futtehabad Allen was disappointed by the attendance at his afternoon service. On 24 October they reached Sultanpore where they were distressed by the unexpected death of Captain Ravenscroft, of the 3rd, he had been wounded at Oba in August and everyone thought he was recovering: he was buried by Allen that night. During the service two Brahmin troopers went unarmed for water about 100yd beyond the guards and were murdered. They always fetched their own water because they could not use that provided by the *beesties* (water carriers) for religious reasons since it was held in cow-leather containers. The enemy were still tailing the army in the hope of plunder and about fifteen of them had been killed that day.

Jalalabad was reached after a journey of 7 miles on 25 October: the miserable weather, the need to rest the animals and to blow up the fortifications entailed a halt there of four nights. They were plagued by earthquakes, a dust storm, rain and continual attacks on the camp. Allen, who became progressively more defensive of his camels as the campaign continued, was infuriated by the insouciance of their drivers: 'who will not take warning, or attend to orders, went with their beasts to the opposite side of the river, that they might plunder while the camels were feeding. They were, of course, attacked, and some killed' (*Diary*, 345). None of Allen's camels or drivers, however, seem to have been lost on this occasion. Lieutenant Chamberlayne, 'who was always ready for action', followed the raiders for 8 miles with 100 of the Shah's irregular horse, killed several Afghans and recovered 22 camels. Allen expressed his pleasure, whilst they were at Jalalabad, at seeing a letter from Lord Ellenborough to the chaplains of the diocese of Calcutta requesting them to hold services of thanksgiving for the successes of the 'army of retribution'.

The army finally left Jalalabad in the afternoon of 29 October, their unusually late departure was presumably caused by the need for Pollock's force to march out first in the morning. They went just 5 miles to Ali Boghan but passed through a reedy, slippery swamp where the camels had to go single file and many of them fell. The cavalry rear-guard under Major Simmonds were tired of the constant harassment that they had endured from the Afghans who tailed them hoping for plunder, so they employed a ruse to disperse them. They usually fled when faced by the cavalry but, on this occasion, Lieutenants Graves and Chamberlayne hid their horse behind a ruined fort while the rest of the army marched by and the Afghans came up thinking that all the rear had passed. The officers and their men suddenly charged out from behind the fort and put the enemy to flight, apart from 150 to 200 who were killed.

The following day, on a march of 10 miles, Skinner's horse in the rear-guard employed the same stratagem against marauders as had been successful the day before and killed nine. It was a Sunday but Allen did not comment on the level of attendance in the mess-tent service. On 1 November they marched through the Khoord Khyber pass to Dukka but neither Pollock's nor Nott's forces were attacked despite the narrowness of the road and the height of the gorge that was commanded by a watch-tower. Presumably the tribes were observing them from above but concluded the difficulties of plundering them were too great to warrant the risk. The main problem for the soldiers was the large number of dead and stinking camels left by the preceding brigades that nearly choked the pass. It was a relief to emerge into a beautiful and fruitful valley; while his tent was being pitched Allen and a friend strolled by the river and played a game of 'duck and drake' and they were glad to rest there during the following day.

Two hard marches followed, to Lundi-Kaneh on 3 November and to Ali Musjid on the 4th, the latter was 'undoubtedly the strongest pass I had seen'. The road to it had been improved (presumably by the British during their occupation) but it was very narrow so any camel that fell had to be rolled over the side since the whole force would otherwise be delayed. 'The Great Cazee', a legendary eighteen-pounder of bronze, ornamented with fantastic beasts and fishes, taken from Jalalabad, was another victim that was blown up at this stage. Allen, who seems to have admired great guns, lamented that General Pollock had not brought along one of the sturdy British gun carriages for it that he had destroyed at Khoord Kabul. As they progressed they encountered numerous bodies of the murdered camp followers from the previous brigades, some were already being devoured by dogs and birds of prey. Allen was particularly upset by the sight of two women, one young and good looking, he again expostulated against the folly that led followers either to go in advance or lag behind leading to these tragedies. The soldiers could see the villages up in the heights from which the marauders had come.

As they advanced they came to a small plain near the village of Lalla Beg where they found a number of dead sepoys. Pollock's force had been rushed in the dark there, two officers, Captain Christie and Ensign Nicholson, had been killed and two mountain guns had been captured. One of the guns was later recovered and two light companies were left there to guard the baggage as it came in. Later Allen had the distressing task of comforting Nicholson's brother, who had survived months of harsh imprisonment at Ghazni only to be reunited with his sibling for a very short time before his death: Allen later conducted the young man's burial service. They camped in the valley beneath the fort of Ali Musjid and waited with apprehension for their camels to arrive. In the meantime Allen was grateful for breakfast and shelter from the sun provided by a lieutenant of the Bombay engineers, one of the few whose baggage had come up. Allen was relieved when all his camels and servants finally arrived in the late afternoon. Ali Musjid was a strategically important fort at the entrance to the Khyber pass from the Punjab that had been held by the British until January 1842. They had been forced to abandon it and fall back on Peshawar since shortage of supplies and the prospect of forcing the pass had reduced the sepoys to a state of near mutiny after the dismal news from Kabul started to arrive.

Pollock's army remained at Ali Musjid the following day as camels were still coming in and were exhausted, some had been standing under their loads without food for twenty-six hours. Many had died and others were carried off by the tribesmen who also fatally wounded two men of the 40th. Allen took advantage of the halt to make a sketch of Ali Musjid (Illustration 18) before part of the fort was blown up during the evening. Captain Coser, the commander, 'imprudently exposing himself', got a broken and lacerated leg from a stone during the explosion. The tribesmen (called Khyberees by the British but also known as Afridis) kept up a fierce fire on the pickets all night. The Khyberees were usually bribed by travellers to allow a safe passage through the passes and their indignation at not being paid was compounded by their hatred of the *kaffir feringhees*.

The 6 November was a Sunday but the march from Ali Musjid to Futtehghur was to be a distressing experience. The Khyberees, 'a much bolder race than any we had previously seen', waited in the hills to attack, firing down on the force. Pickets from the native infantry, later supported by a company, climbed up and pursued them and a fierce fight ensued. Allen could not see all the action because of a bend in the road but skirmishing in the rear continued for the rest of the march through the pass. His friend and hero, Lieutenant Terry of the Bombay artillery, was mortally wounded by a ball in the chest and the audacious Lieutenant Chamberlayne received his sixth wound of the campaign in the leg: it was to be one of the last shots fired in the war.

Eventually the army:

came in sight of the wide plains of the Punjab, extending to the horizon. At sight of this, the sepoys of the light companies, who were in front, set up a deafening cheer; and most fully did we all participate in their joy. By degrees we cleared the hills, and came down upon the Sik fort of Futtehghur, leaving Jumrood to the right. Men were sitting by the road-side, selling grain and sweetmeats, and, when we pitched our camp, women were soon crying milk in the lines. These were strange sights to us, who had been for months without seeing a human being, except as an enemy.

(Diary, 359)

Allen held his usual service in the mess tent and, mindful of their losses and their joy at returning to India, preached on the text from Psalm ciii, 17–18, 'But the mercy of the Lord is from everlasting to everlasting upon them that fear him.'

The journey was uneventful for the next few days except for the death of Lieutenant Terry who had been sinking since he was wounded in the pass: Allen had sat with him when he could. He was on his way to Terry's tent on the morning of 9 November but met the doctor who said that he had died after stressing how comforting he had found Allen's presence, he had asked with his last breath that the clergyman should be sent for. Terry was buried that evening before a large number of grieving officers.

The army reached Peshawar on 12 November and camped about 4½ miles outside. From there it moved off towards British India in brigades but, as General Nott's division formed the rear as it had done since leaving Kabul, Allen and the 40th stayed there for several days. General Avitabile, the hospitable Neapolitan governor for the Maharajah of the Punjab, kept open house for the British officers. Allen enjoyed a splendid breakfast at his residence on 14 November: 'About forty guests were present. The general, who had been out for a morning drive, returned in a carriage drawn by four mules, with a large retinue running on foot, one of whom carried an immense umbrella over his head. He is a tall, stout, elderly man, exceedingly affable' (*Diary*, 361).

After breakfast the general gave his guests an escort so they could see the town. Allen was not impressed by it and disliked the sight of the bodies of many executed criminals hanging from gibbets. He concluded from this and from the manner of the guards that Avitabile was a very severe ruler: but he had told them that without such severity he could not maintain his position. In his defence, Allen said that every night, he had a box lowered from his residence into which the inhabitants of Peshawar were invited to place grievances or petitions. The death of Ranjit Singh in 1839 had left the Punjab in a particularly volatile condition, so the general's strong rule provided at least one area of stable government. Avitabile was greatly feared not just by the Sikhs but also by the Afghans, as Mackenzie remarked he was: 'spoken of by the Afghan population with the admiration of a troop of jackals for a tiger' (Macrory, 129).

Nott's division marched through the Punjab without incident and crossed on the river Indus at Attock by a bridge made of boats on 18 November: they had several more rivers to cross before they reached Ferozepore but these were traversed in rather than on boats. Before describing their festive reception there Allen paused to castigate the 'unworthy and unwearied scribblers' who had attached themselves to the army since it left Afghanistan and who, especially in the Indian newspapers, denigrated what it had achieved. Under the cover of anonymity they exaggerated every reverse to the extent that they represented the campaign as a retreat by a diseased and demoralised force in the course of which all sorts of atrocities had been committed. Allen indignantly opposed these views with his account of the successful, orderly and professional way in which the army had left the country.

Allen had mixed feelings about the army's reception on 23 December by Lord Ellenborough at Ferozepore: on the one hand it was faintly ridiculous, on the other he was impressed by the splendour and even rode back behind the rear of the cavalry lining the ceremonial route so he could see the rest of the force march past. They had:

> arrived at a noble bridge of boats, decorated with the colours of 'the ribbon of India', red, yellow and blue. At the farther end we passed under a kind of canopy of the same colours, ornamented at the top with flags. On leaving this we entered a long and glittering street formed of native cavalry, at the head of which were the governor-general, the commander-in-chief, and multitudes of aides-de-camp, etc., composing their staff, in every variety of uniform, and ladies upon enormous elephants, with *howdahs* (seats on elephants' backs) richly caparisoned; crimson and yellow were the prevailing colours, the latter distinguishing the numerous Sik troops who were present.
>
> (*Diary*, 369)

After the soldiers had passed Allen was sorry to observe the 'child-like parade' of the gates of the temple of Somnath, more likely to excite 'the ridicule of reflecting natives' than improve their opinion of Britain. Ever since he arrived at the frontier to Afghanistan in the early months of 1842 he had been all too conscious of the great blow that the army's defeat there had delivered to the Indians' view of their rulers. This was one reason why he was so indignant about adverse press reports that questioned the success of 'the army of retribution'.

Considering the long months, and in some cases years, that the soldiers had been away from their bases in India, Allen thought that they had managed to look remarkably smart during the parade, although close inspection would have shown patches and other repairs. In contrast to the fresh soldiers who had come up with the Governor General, however, they were shabby although this was regarded as a badge of honour. A man of the 40th passing an aide-de-camp resplendent in crimson, gold lace and plumes remarked to a mate: 'Ah Jack that chap has never come through the Khyber, that's quite evident' (*Diary*, 371).

In the evening the Governor General held a grand dinner for the senior officers, including General Nott and Major Hibbert of the 40th. The tent was so enormous that it could only be put in place by elephants, and even they laboured under the load: a hundred people altogether sat down to eat. It was splendidly lit and carpeted and Allen, who was apparently one of the guests, appreciated the compliments that Ellenborough (not usually a pleasant man) paid to General Nott and Major Hibbert.

All kinds of celebrations took place during the following days in the huge camp that contained about 40,000 soldiers and 3 times that number of camp followers, so it was impressive that they were all well supplied with provisions. Allen was gratified that, despite his cloth, he was given a campaign medal when the plentiful honours were being distributed. On Christmas Day he held a service for the Kandahar force, assembled in the centre street of the camp. The text of his sermon was Luke, ii, 11–14, 'I bring you good tidings of great joy.' He drew a contrast with the previous Christmas and the day on which he was preaching:

In what depressing gloom must this holy season have been spent by our unhappy countrymen, but a few days before they commenced that disastrous retreat which glutted with their flesh the birds and beasts of the savage region through which they attempted to penetrate, and paved its passes with their whitening bones, when they contrasted their hopeless misery, among sanguinary foes, with the congratulations and smiles of friends, the gladness and joy, which were accustomed to greet them on the same anniversary, in the far distant land of their birth! How painful and agonizing a period it was to us, who received from day to day the appalling but alas! not exaggerated rumours of their sufferings and destruction!

(*Diary*, 444)

Allen concluded by exhorting his congregation not to succumb to the temptations of the peace and prosperity that they were enjoying but to spend the holy season living as good Christians. Ever conscientious, he then assisted Reverend Whiting, the Governor General's chaplain, at a service that was attended by Lord Ellenborough, Sir Jasper Nicholls, senior and junior officers, many of whom took Holy Communion. In the afternoon, as usual, he held a service in the mess tent of the 40th.

With his new friend, the Reverend Whiting, Allen spent another interesting day on 31 December at a private *durbar* given to receive Dhyan Singh, the young heir to the Punjab. The ten-year-old and his retinue were richly dressed and the boy seemed to stagger under the weight of the jewels that he was wearing. The effect was somewhat spoilt, however, in Allen's opinion by the dirty stockings from which their toes protruded when they removed their shoes. They then watched a great review of about 30,000 from the back of an elephant, a new experience for Allen. He could not resist pointing out to Whiting the colours of the 40th as it passed, 'decorated with the names of almost all our great victories from Egypt downwards'.

In the evening Allen attended a farewell dinner that was given by the 3rd to their friends the 40th. The skies opened as he rode there and he and all the other guests arrived soaked to the skin. They were given dry clothing but the rain penetrated the canvas mess tent and, as the camp was situated on a flat plain, they were soon sitting ankle-deep in water. He got a litter for his return but its canvas cover was no protection and it was like sitting under a shower-bath. He pitied the soldiers and followers whose belongings were floating about everywhere and, as the troops had no bedsteads, they had to stand all night with their bedding over their shoulders. Allen was relieved to find that when he eventually reached his tent it was dry as his careful servants had dug a trench round it.

The army began to disperse and it was time for Allen to return to civilian life. He left the camp at Ferozepore at the same time as Major Hibbert, Lieutenant Seymour and other friends from the 40th on 9 January 1843. Over *tiffin* several officers tried to make farewell speeches but they were overcome with emotion. The band played as the major and his companions rode out through the lines and all the troops spontaneously put on their uniforms and turned out to cheer them, 'One cheer more for the major!', 'One cheer more for the minister!' They followed the officers for 2 miles out of the camp cheering, weeping, shaking their hands and blessing them whilst the officers were so overcome that they found it difficult to respond with their thanks.

Allen travelled back to Sukkur and from there retraced his journey by boat to Hyderabad with Major Outram (see Part II, Chapter I). Allen then went on to Tatta with Major Wade of the 13th and so to Karachi where his adventure had started. The two had travelled without an escort and, had they realised it, were in considerable danger since shortly after their departure from Hyderabad, Outram had fought and won a battle there for the defence of the residency. The Baluchis were assembling for the beginning of the conflict that was to end in the British annexation of Sind and would almost certainly have murdered Allen and Wade if they had encountered them.

After an absence from Bombay of one year and ten months, Allen reached it by boat on 26 February 1843. He hoped that his readers had found his narrative interesting and assured them that he had written nothing but the truth. He had not: 'hesitated to express censure where I thought it deserved, and have felt it equally a duty to repel unmerited reproach' (*Diary*, 381). He trusted that it would make his readers feel grateful to the

Almighty for the great mercies that he had shown to the British through the trials that they had endured. Allen's claim to truthfulness is born out by a comparison of his *Diary* with other contemporary accounts, letters and government papers. He was a witness to many of the episodes in the later stages of the war and seems to have reported them faithfully, often leavening them with a gentle humour. Given that he was new to the country, did not speak any Asian languages and was not senior enough to be privy to some information, his account is impressive.

Conclusion

Lady Sale and the Reverend Allen had both deplored the bad judgement by the government in Britain and India that had led to the war and then the way in which it had been conducted in Afghanistan by General Elphinstone and Brigadier Shelton. Lord Auckland, the Governor General who planned and supported the campaign, must bear much of the responsibility for its failure in the winter of 1841/2 mainly because he had prevailed upon the wildly unsuitable Elphinstone to take command. Afterwards Ellenborough, the Governor General from February 1842, made his contempt for his predecessor plain but hesitated for several months before he allowed the reinforcements Auckland had ordered up from India to leave Jalalabad and Kandahar. This caused unnecessary delays in the rescue of the British prisoners and in establishing 'the accustomed superiority of the British arms' in Afghanistan.

As both Lady Sale and Allen anticipated, the impact of British defeat on opinion in India had been devastating. The 'unworthy and unwearied' scribblers from the British and Indian press proved as deadly to the soldiers in the field as their counterparts have sometimes been (with the exception of those who are actually out there with the soldiers) in the current conflict in Afghanistan. Even in the early months of her imprisonment Lady Sale was receiving reports of all sorts of libels and inaccuracies that found their way into the press and Allen became positively apoplectic with indignation at what he heard and read. Many factors contributed to the outbreak of the Indian Mutiny in 1857 but one was that the British army had shown that it was not invincible when it was defeated in Afghanistan in the winter of 1841/2 (David, 49–50) and another the perception that 'the army of retribution' had made a disorderly retreat in the autumn of the latter year. Allen's *Diary* and other accounts by soldiers involved in the campaign make it clear that the army left Afghanistan in a disciplined military fashion, punishing those who were foolish enough to attack and attempt to plunder it.

Native Indian indignation at the abandonment of many sepoys and camp followers by the army was more justified. On the one hand General Nott seems to have made little effort to take former prisoners and slaves back with him, on the other General Pollock took 2,000 and that may have been near the total of those who wished to return. Some (including perhaps Europeans) had been abducted or sold into slavery in areas the army could not penetrate and some had deserted and may have preferred to take their chances in Afghanistan. The impact of these losses of their fellow countrymen and women on Indian opinion, however, was disastrous and must count as another cause of the Mutiny. Twenty-three out of the twenty-four Bengal Native Infantry and Cavalry regiments that had served in Afghanistan either mutinied or were disbanded in 1857 (Whitteridge, 138).

British opinion in the late summer of 1842, before news had arrived of the fall of Kabul and the release of the prisoners, was probably well summarised by Greville:

> The Whig papers are attacking Ellenborough [a Tory appointment] with the greatest asperity and doing all they can to divert public attention from the original expedition and its subsequent disasters [under the Whigs], and to fix the general indignation upon him for the policy he is disposed to adopt . . . the [Tory] Government have made up their minds to renounce all idea of permanent conquests and establishment in Afghanistan. The English Public will be satisfied if they get back the prisoners, which is what they think most about, and though they will be dissatisfied and disappointed if some sort of vengeance is not executed upon Akbar Khan, they will on the whole be happy to be extricated from such an embarrassing and expensive scrape.

(11 September 1842, Norris, 429)

The irony behind this sentiment is that, far from disengaging from the North West Frontier, Britain was to conquer and annex both Sind and the Punjab during the remainder of the decade.

* * *

The leading characters in the version of the war in 1842 that has been described above were to enjoy mixed fortunes. The Sales were feted when they returned to Britain at a number of receptions, including one given by Queen Victoria. They even figured in Astley's circus where Lady Sale was shown flourishing a sword and leading the troops during the retreat from Kabul. They could have retired comfortably and full of honours, but 'Fighting Bob' could not resist participating in the First Sikh War. He had been promoted to the rank of quarter-master general of the Queen's troops in the East Indies and did not need to lead his soldiers into battle. He nevertheless did so and was mortally wounded at the battle of Moodki on 21 December 1845: he died soon afterwards and was buried on the field (Illustrations 19, 20). The *Morning Chronicle* published a memorial poem that finished:

> A fame is his no fame can dim
>
> No time can ever pale-
>
> Who would not die and live like him
>
> The brave Sir Robert Sale

(Sale-Hill, 23)

Lady Sale retired on a good pension of £500 a year to Simla but her health declined to such an extent that she went to South Africa in the hope of a cure. She died in Cape Town on 6 July 1853 and her tombstone bears the inscription: 'Underneath this stone reposes all that could die of Lady Sale' (Sale, ed. Macrory, 159). Alexandrina Sturt remained in India and married Major James Garner Holmes, commander of the 12th Irregular Bengal Cavalry, as her second husband. They were in the wrong place early in the Mutiny on 24 July 1857, taking an evening drive in their carriage at Segowli, Patna District, when four sowars (native cavalrymen) seized and beheaded them both.

The Reverend Allen lived a peaceful life after his return to Bombay: he first went to Deesa and then, in 1845, to Poona. He married Mary Anne Brown, aged thirty-one, in that year and they had four children, three girls and a boy. He was promoted from assistant to full chaplain but, apart from publishing *Reflections on Portions of the Sermon on the Mount*, a long two-part tract intended for soldiers in 1848, he seems not to have distinguished himself. It has been suggested above that his independence of mind and habit of speaking plainly probably did not improve his career prospects. He died at Poona at the age of forty-four in 1855 and was buried there: his widow survived until the age of eighty three.

General Nott did not live long to reap the rewards of his successes in Afghanistan. He was appointed in 1843 to the prestigious post of resident at the court of Oudh and was invested with the GCB on Ellenborough's recommendation, for he believed that he had been the ablest general who had fought in the war. Nott had been a widower for some time and re-married in June 1843, but recurrent heart disease forced him to go on leave to Britain in the following year. He was too ill even to accept an invitation to meet Queen Victoria at Windsor and died at his home in Carmarthen on 1 January 1845.

It was normal practice to subject senior officers who had been captured and imprisoned to a court martial and this was Brigadier Shelton's fate. Surprisingly, he was acquitted on three of the four charges that were brought against him. He was only found guilty of trying to obtain forage from Akbar Khan whilst negotiations with Sir William Macnaghten were being held. No further action was taken against him as the court believed that he had been censured by General Elphinstone at the time. Shelton returned to Britain to command the re-constituted HM 44th Regiment of Foot but died in Dublin after a fall from his horse in 1845. On receiving the news his regiment turned out on the parade ground 'and gave three hearty cheers' (Macrory, 270).

Captain Colin Mackenzie continued to practise his brand of evangelical Christianity with fervour. He never found favour with the Indian government, which was strongly prejudiced against political agents, although he was eventually promoted to the rank of lieutenant-general and was awarded a CB. He retired to Britain in 1873 and wrote to the newspapers five years later strongly opposing the British intervention that led to the Second Afghan War. He died in Edinburgh in 1881. Captain George Lawrence and his brother Henry both went on to enjoy glittering careers in the Indian army and civil service. George served with distinction in the Second Sikh War and was then chief agent for the Governor General in Rajputana where he retained the loyalty of the princes during the Mutiny. He was promoted to the rank of major-general in 1861, retired five years later and died in London in 1884.

Lieutenant Eyre's description of the hostilities, his subsequent imprisonment and the sketches he made were published at the same time as Lady Sale's and the Reverend Allen's in 1843. While the latter seems to have sunk without trace, Eyre enhanced his reputation with his account and enjoyed a distinguished career. His valiant actions during the Mutiny led to him being recommended for a Victoria Cross and he was promoted to the rank of lieutenant-general in 1863 when he retired. He happened to be in France during the Franco-Prussian War and successfully organised an ambulance service. His health later deteriorated and he was in Aix-les-Bains in France when he died in 1881.

Major Eldred Pottinger, the renowned defender of Herat and the man mainly responsible for freeing the prisoners without a fight, ended his promising career miserably. Lord Ellenborough's dislike of political agents meant that no post was offered to him when he returned to India. Rather than go back to Britain, he accepted an invitation to Hong Kong, which had recently become a colony and where his uncle, Sir Henry Pottinger, was the governor; but 'the hero of Herat' died there of typhus shortly after his arrival.

Shah Dost Mohammed was released by the British and returned to Kabul to re-occupy his throne in 1843. He ruled firmly and, in contrast to Shah Shujah, was reasonably popular with his subjects. He lived until 1863, rather longer than his favourite son, Akbar Khan, who died at Jalalabad (possibly from poison) in 1847. Until relations deteriorated in the 1870s, the regime was generally friendly with the British and kept its distance from the Russians.

The accounts left by a number of the participants in the war enjoyed a flourishing afterlife. Lady Sale became an instant celebrity through her letters from Afghanistan and the publication of her *Journal*. Her fame has continued, especially since the allies became involved in a war against the Taliban and al-Qaeda in 2001. The Tricycle Theatre in London, for

167

example, staged a series of short plays, a film festival entitled *The Great Game* and a display of Afghan contemporary pottery and photography in 2009. The first play in the series, *Bugles at the Gates of Jalalabad* by Stephen Jeffreys, featured Lady Sale. She has become something of a feminist icon, despite her failings (she never reported anything that might be discreditable to her husband). Annabel Venning observed: 'Stoical though she undoubtedly was, seldom complaining even when racked with fever or with pain from her wound, Lady Sale cannot have been the easiest of companions. Tall and imposing with a habit of speaking her mind, she was also inclined to be selfish' (Venning, 280). Apart from Captain Mackenzie, the officers who left accounts of the First Afghan War have tended to the 'stiff upper lip' school of writing, whilst Lady Sale's account sparkles with its candour, humanity and grim humour.

Unlike Lady Sale's *Journal*, the *Diary* of the Reverend Allen appears to have exercised no appreciable influence over opinion concerning the war. The British government in India and the East India Company had an ambivalent attitude towards the Anglican Church, for whilst they saw that it was needed to minister to the European community they were afraid of offending native susceptibilities. Allen was too junior and obscure to carry any weight and his sometimes vehement opinions, if they were known, probably only caused mild irritation on the part of his employers. For modern readers, however, his frank views about the good and bad aspects of the campaign of 1842, on the Afghans and his warm admiration for the courage, generosity and camaraderie he encountered in the army are still relevant.

* * *

Finally, what parallels can be drawn with the present-day war in Afghanistan? Throughout this book evidence about Afghan methods of fighting, attitudes towards foreigners and political activities has been cited. Some things may have changed by the early twenty-first century but recent experience indicates that many have not. Lady Sale was not the only writer to observe that, although the Afghans could rarely face a disciplined force in the field, they were well equipped for guerrilla warfare. Their advantage was compounded by the fact that the British troops had poor quality muskets, as Lieutenant Greenwood complained, that were inferior to the Afghan *jezails* in practically every respect: remarks about defective or even missing equipment that will resonate with today's soldiers.

Military measures that might have been effective in Europe had little impact: villages and forts might be blown up as reprisals but the tough, impoverished population simply took to the hills, returned when the army moved on and rebuilt their mud and stone dwellings. The terrain in which the armies operated was totally unforgiving: whether they were entering or leaving Afghanistan from or to their bases in India they had to march through some of the most difficult and dangerous mountain passes in the world enduring extreme temperatures, both hot and cold. The Afghans had centuries of experience of taking advantage of these features. Heavy British guns, which were effective in defending Kandahar and Jalalabad, were a terrible burden to the army and its draught animals in the passes. The twenty-first-century war is being mainly conducted in plains and deserts but there too the local population have the advantage of knowing the terrain well. The allied forces attempting to flush out their enemies in the wild borderlands with Pakistan probably encounter conditions that would have been familiar to the armies of the nineteenth century.

Until the First Afghan War the majority of the population were suspicious of foreigners and actively hostile to *kaffirs*, although minorities such as the Hazaras or Kuzzilbashis could see advantages in co-operating with the rich and powerful British, especially if they could assist them against their enemies. The war changed the attitude of the majority since they perceived the invasion as unjustified aggression against their nation, made worse by the installation by force of an unpopular king in Kabul. The presence of an infidel army in that city, in Kandahar, Ghazni and other fortresses was a blow to national pride and to Islam. The people have long memories, according to Macrory garbled but passionate versions of the British defeats in 1841/4, 1878/80 and 1919 were still being told in the 1960s. One old man claimed to the American anthropologist Louis Dupree that he was the grandson of Mahommed Shah Khan, the prisoners' gaoler in the Laghman valley (Macrory, 278–80). Apart from the Russians, the British are probably still the least-welcome people in Afghanistan. As General Roberts remarked after the Second Afghan War, 'the less the Afghans see us the less they will dislike us'.

Given the bitterness with which most Afghans of all orders regarded the occupying forces, it is not surprising that, in November and December 1841 and January 1842, they exploited British vulnerability. Allen observed that Afghans would attack when the enemy was weak but retreat when he was strong: Elphinstone, Nott and, to some extent Sale, demonstrated both aspects of this tendency. Nott gained respect from his enemies by his harsh measures against them, Sale after a determined defence of Jalalabad, wobbled in March but wiser counsels prevailed and steadied his resolve, the gentle Elphinstone succumbed to the wiles of his enemies with disastrous results. In Kabul and on the retreat the British leaders persisted in believing the promises of Akbar Khan and his followers, applying Western, Christian rules of conduct in a situation that they could not control. Until it was too late they did not comprehend that Afghan negotiators who might be polite, offer them tea and make attractive promises were deliberately lying and glorying in doing so. They saw absolutely nothing wrong in conducting such negotiations: internal feuding was endemic in their society and there was no shame in successfully deceiving a member of a rival tribe or family, still less *kaffirs*. Akbar himself seems to have suffered from this situation in the spring of 1842 when he could trust only a few allies and relatives amongst the chiefs. There are signs that the Western allies in the twenty-first century are beginning to understand the mindset of their adversaries and recognise these cultural differences in their dealings with them.

Bribes paid to the Ghilzai chiefs had been an important factor in ensuring the relative stability of Shah Shujah's rule for his first two years and it is often said that the revolt of November 1841 was caused by the reduction in those payments. During the retreat the British offered their tormentors large sums (admittedly mainly in promissory notes since most of the gold had been stolen) but were told that the tribesmen hated the *kaffirs* so intensely that no amount of money could save their lives. Time will tell whether or not using Western money to build up the infrastructure, wean farmers away from the opium poppy (one problem the British did not encounter in mid-nineteenth-century Afghanistan) and the Taliban away from their guns will work in the early twenty-first century. One lesson, however, that can be learnt from the First Afghan War is that it is better to spend money from a position of strength than of weakness.

At the beginning of this book it was suggested, and this is supported by evidence from Allen and the other officers who kept journals, that the return to India in the autumn of 1842 was not a disorderly retreat but a disciplined withdrawal. Had the British government wished to keep an army in Afghanistan they could probably have done so but the cost in lives and treasure would have been very high. Since there was no evidence of the Russian influence that they had feared and Dost Mohammed showed no signs of wishing to revenge himself (and this was proved by his conduct during the Indian Mutiny), there was no good reason for the British to remain. Parallels may be found with the allied situation at the beginning of the second decade of this century. The US, Britain and their allies wish to withdraw from Afghanistan as soon as possible, but until they believe that they leave behind a government that is strong enough to ensure that the Taliban and their friends in al-Qaeda do not permanently establish themselves as a major force, they cannot do so. The situation ten years ago is not comparable to the prelude to the First Afghan War since terrorist activities really did present a threat to the West. The price paid by the people of Afghanistan and all the combatants during the last decade has been a high one, but if allied armed forces and politicians can achieve peace and stability it may just have been worth it. One resource available to them in these difficult times is the knowledge acquired by the armies and their historians from the previous wars in Afghanistan.

Glossary

Some Hindi and Pashto words are given as they are spelt by Lady Sale and the Reverend Allen. Words frequently used by the British such as 'sepoy' are not italicised in the text.

Amir ruler
Assassins fanatical Shia sect that arose in Syria and Persia in the eleventh century
Ayah nurse
Bahadur mighty or boastful
Batta extra army pay
Beestie water carrier
Bourj tower
Bunder quay or harbour
Burka full-body covering worn outdoors by Muslim ladies
Cantonment semi-permanent military station
CB Companion of the Order of the Bath
Chappati bread
Charpoy bed made with ropes stretched from poles
Chillumchee washbasin
Conductor NCO charged with obtaining army supplies
Cossid messenger
Doolie litter
Durbar meeting
Factory merchant's trading station
Fakir holy beggar
Feringhee foreigner
GCB Knight Grand Cross of the Order of the Bath

Ghazi fanatical Muslim

Ghee liquid butter

Griffin young man freshly arrived from Britain

Harem enclosed women's quarters in Muslim houses

Hookah pipe where the smoke is drawn through water

Houris beautiful maidens in paradise

Howdah seat on an elephant's back

Jemadar native army lieutenant

Jezail long Afghan rifle

Jezailchi rifleman

Kaffir infidel

KCB Knight Commander of the Order of the Bath

Kuzzilbashi red-haired, Afghan of Persian origin

Lakh £10,000 worth of rupees

Matchlock Afghan rifle

Mirza secretary

Mugger crocodile

Mullah priest

Musjid mosque

Naick native corporal

Nazir steward

NCO non-commissioned officer

Nemchee sheepskin waistcoat

Nullah bed of a river

Oorsee open-work lattices

Palkee camel pannier

Pariah vagabond dogs

Pinnace small ship accompanying a larger vessel

Poshteen fur-lined Afghan coat

Puggeree turban

Sace groom

Salaam greeting

Seer equivalent to 2lb in weight

Sepoy native infantryman

Shikarghur hunting ground
Sirdar general
Sowar native cavalryman
Sungah breastwork
Tank man-made lake or pond
Tiffin lunch
Tykana cellar or basement
Wuzeer vizier
Yaboo pony

List of Characters

Abbott, Captain Augustus, artillery officer with Nott, his correspondence was published in 1879

Achilles, Greek hero of the Trojan War

Aga Mohammed Khan, a pro-British Kuzzilbashi prince

Ahmed Shah, founder of the Durrani monarchy in the eighteenth century

Alexander the Great (Sikunder), ruler of fourth century BC, renowned in Afghanistan

Ali Mohammed Khan, a Kuzzilbashi gaoler of the prisoners

Allen, Reverend Isaac Nicholson, chaplain to Nott's army, his *Diary* was published in 1843

Alston, Captain James, a defender of Ghazni, prisoner

Anderson, Mary, 'Tootsey', young daughter of Captain William and Mrs Anderson, kidnapped on the retreat from Kabul, were all then prisoners with their other children

Anquetil, Brigadier Thomas, killed on retreat from Kabul

Apthorpe, Major Frederick, mortally wounded at Haikalzai, 28 March 1842

Auckland, Lord (George Eden), Governor General of India until February 1842

Avitabile, Paolo di, Neapolitan general in Sikh service, Governor of Peshawar

Baness, Mr, a Greek merchant who died after reaching Jalalabad, January 1842

Babur, Emperor, founder of the Moghul Empire, died in 1530

Batti Dusd, 'Batti the thief', Mackenzie's guide to Jalalabad

Berwick, Dr, left in Kabul to care for the sick, prisoner

Blewitt, Mr, a clerk, prisoner

Boyd, Captain, chief commissariat officer, and Mrs Boyd and two children, prisoners, when she had another baby

Boyd, Major, quarter-master general to General England's force

Brett, Lieutenant Henry, artillery officer in England's force

Broadfoot, Captain George, an engineer, part of Sale's force

Broadfoot, Lieutenant William, brother to the above, killed with Burnes in Kabul, 2 November 1841

Bryce, Dr Alexander, killed on the retreat from Kabul

Brydon, Dr William, Shah's service, the only European officer from the army to reach Jalalabad after the retreat

Burnes, Sir Alexander, British Resident, murdered in Kabul, 2 November 1841

Burnes, Lieutenant Charles, killed with his older brother

Burnes, Mrs, a soldier's wife (Lady Sale calls her 'Burnes' but in Appendix III to the 1969 edition of her *Journal* only a 'Mrs Bourne' is cited; a Mrs Bourne, but no Mrs Burnes, is mentioned by Captain Mackenzie)

Bury, Captain Horatio, cavalry officer killed at Oba, 28 August 1842

Bygrave, Captain Bulstrode, paymaster, prisoner

Campbell, William, a Eurasian mercenary leading his own regiment in the service of Shah Shujah, later served Dost Mohammed

Campbell, Dr, prisoner

Cardew, Dr Edward, killed on the retreat from Kabul

Carey, Lieutenant Robert, in Nott's force

Chamberlayne, Lieutenant, cavalry with Nott at Kandahar

Chambers, Colonel Robert, killed on retreat from Kabul

Christie, Captain, killed during Pollock's march from Kabul, 4 November 1842

Conolly, Lieutenant John, hostage, died of fever in captivity

Conolly, Captain Arthur, brother of above, executed in Bokhara, June 1842

Coser, Captain, wounded at Ali Musjid by his own explosion

Craigie, Captain Patrick, with Nott, held Kalat-i-Ghilzai until abandoned by British

Deane, Sergeant, killed on the retreat from Kabul

Deane, Mrs, widow of the above, forcibly married to an Afghan

Delamaine, Captain Charles, cavalry officer in Nott's army

Dennie, Colonel William, killed in battle at Jalalabad, 7 April 1842

Dhyan Singh, heir to the Punjab

Dost Mohammed Shah, of the Barukzai dynasty, ruler of Kabul

Dost Mohammed Khan Ghilzai, brother of Mohammed Shah Khan

Drummond, Captain, hostage in Kabul

Ellenborough, Lord (Edward Law), Governor General of India from February 1842

Elphinstone, Major General William CB, commander of the British army in Afghanistan, died in captivity

Elphinstone, Mountstuart, Governor of Bombay and writer

England, Major General Richard, reinforced Nott at Kandahar

Evans, Lieutenant William, in command of the sick left at Kabul, prisoner

Ewart, Major, killed on retreat from Kabul

Eyre, Lieutenant Vincent, artillery, an amateur artist and keeper of a journal, his wife and child, prisoners

Fallon, Mr, a clerk, prisoner

Futteh Jung, a son of Shah Shujah, who succeeded him briefly in Kabul

Gleig, Reverend G.R., Principal Chaplain to the Forces, author of many history books

Graves, Lieutenant, a cavalry officer serving with Nott

Greenwood, Lieutenant Joseph, part of Pollock's force, wrote an account that was published in 1844

Greville, Charles, diarist

Griffiths, Major Charles, prisoner

Haldane, Captain, cavalry, part of Nott's army

Harris, Lieutenant Charles, a defender of Ghazni, then a prisoner

Haughton, Lieutenant John, wounded at Sharikar and later a prisoner

Havelock, Captain Henry, with Sale at Jalalabad, later became a distinguished general

Hibbert, Major later Lieutenant Colonel George, commander of HM 40th Regiment of Foot in Nott's army

Holmes, Major James Garner, commander of 12th Bengal Irregular Native Cavalry, second husband of Alexandrina Sturt, killed with his wife during the Indian Mutiny

Jacob, Captain Mackenzie's Indian, Christian servant, prisoner

Johnson, Captain Hugh, prisoner, kept journals

Keane, Lieutenant General Sir John, commander of the 'army of the Indus'

Knox, Lieutenant John Samuel, interpreter and quarter-master to General Nott's force, author of a journal

Lane, Colonel Charles, served with Nott and fought a victorious defensive action at Kandahar

Lawrence, Captain George, a political agent and prisoner, kept a journal

Lawrence, Captain Henry, brother of above, part of 'army of retribution'

Leech, Major Robert, a political agent

Leeson, Captain Joseph in Nott's army

Leslie, Captain John, officer of horse artillery under England's and then Nott's command

Lewis, Corporal, captured on retreat and forced to convert to Islam, released by Captains Mackenzie and Troup

Lisson, Sergeant Major, released after capture on retreat to take a message to Jalalabad

Lord, Dr, political agent at Bamian, killed in action in 1840

McCaskill, General, commanding rear in General Pollock's march from Kabul

Macdonald, Hester, an unmarried girl, prisoner

Macgrath, Mr John, a surgeon, prisoner

Macgregor, Captain George, political agent at Jalalabad

Mackenzie, Captain Colin, a political agent and prisoner

Maclaren, Colonel James, failed to relieve Kabul from Kandahar in early December 1841

Maclean, Captain Archibald and Mrs, Allen's hosts at Sukkur

Macnaghten, Sir William, British government envoy murdered in Kabul, 23 December 1842

Macnaghten, Lady Fanny, wife/widow of Sir William, prisoner

Mahmood of Ghazni, revered military and religious Afghan leader of eleventh century

Mainwaring, Lieutenant James, part of Nott's garrison at Kandahar

Mainwaring, Mrs, and baby, a prisoner and wife of a captain in the Jalalabad garrison

May, Captain William, part of England's force, killed at Haikalzai, 28 March 1842

Melville, Lieutenant Henry, prisoner

Mien, Lieutenant George, prisoner

Mohammed Akbar Khan, favourite son of Dost Mohammed Shah

Mohammed Shah Khan Ghilzai, one of Akbar Khan's fathers-in-law

Mohammed Zahir Shah, King of Afghanistan until 1973

Mohan Lal, a Hindu interpreter working for the British in Kabul

Montieth, Colonel Thomas, part of Sale's force

Nicholl, Captain Thomas, killed on the retreat from Kabul

Nicholls, Sir Jasper, commander-in-chief of the British forces in India

Nicholson, Lieutenant John, a defender of Ghazni then a prisoner

Nicholson, Ensign Alexander, younger brother of the above, killed on march from Kabul, 4 November 1842

Nott, Major General Sir William GCB, commander of the Kandahar garrison and one of the armies that took Kabul

Outram, Major James, political agent at Dadur

Palmer, Colonel Thomas, defender of Ghazni, captured and imprisoned

Peel, Sir Robert, Conservative Prime Minister

Piggot, Reverend George, chaplain to 'the army of the Indus', 1838/9 and founder of the Afghan Church at Colabah, Bombay

Pollock, Major General Sir George GCB, commander of the 'army of retribution'

Pottinger, Major Eldred, political agent and prisoner

Ranjit Singh, Maharajah of the Punjab until 1839

Ravenscroft, Captain George, cavalry, part of Nott's army, wounded at Oba and died on march back to India

Rawlinson, Major Henry, political agent at Kandahar

Reeves, Captain George, cavalry, killed at Oba, 28 August 1842

Reynolds, Sergeant, died of lockjaw whilst a prisoner

Riley, Mr, a conductor of ordnance, wife and three children, prisoners

Sale, Lady Florentia, wife of General Sale and a prisoner who kept a journal

Sale, Major-General Sir Robert, KCB, commander of the Jalalabad garrison

Saleh Mohammed Khan, gaoler bribed to release prisoners at Bamian

Scott, Lieutenant James, Pollock's army, mortally sick in Kabul, October 1842

Seymour, Lieutenant Henry, part of England's and then Nott's army

Shahpoor, young son of Shah Shujah, left in Kabul by the army in October 1842

Shah Shujah-al-Mukh, of the Sadozai dynasty, a former ruler of Afghanistan restored by the British in 1839, murdered in April 1842

Shakespear, Colonel Sir Richmond, Pollock's military secretary, sent to rescue the prisoners

Shelton, Brigadier John, colonel of HM 44th Regiment of Foot, prisoner

Shumshoodeen Khan, the chief who held Ghazni

Simmonds, Major Joseph, serving under England then Nott

Skinner, Captain James, killed on the retreat from Kabul

Smith, Mrs, widow, servant of Mrs Trevor, died in prison

Smith, Mrs, wife of a collector, murdered in Bolan Pass, October 1841

Souter, Captain Thomas, prisoner

Stacey, Brigadier Lewis, commanded second brigade on Nott's march to Kabul

Stoddart, Colonel Charles, executed in Bokhara, June 1842

Stoker, Seymour, a small child orphaned on the retreat and died after being abducted by Mrs Wade

Stuart, Captain Thomas, his wife and family, friends of Allen from Karachi

Sturt, Alexandrina Mrs, daughter of Sales, whilst a prisoner gave birth to a daughter

Sturt, Captain John, engineer, married to Alexandrina, killed on the retreat from Kabul

Sufter Jung, a renegade son of Shah Shujah

Sultan Jan, a cousin and supporter of Akbar Khan

Taj Mohammed Khan, a pro-British Afghan chief

Terry, Lieutenant Walter, artillery officer with Nott's army, fatally wounded in the Khyber Pass

Thain, Major William, killed on the retreat from Kabul

Thomas, Captain Alfred, accompanied Reverend Allen as far as Shikarpore

Timur Shah, oldest son of Shah Shujah, returned to India with Pollock

Trevor, Captain Robert, murdered with Macnaghten in Kabul, 23 December 1842

Trevor, Mrs, wife/widow of Captain Trevor, who had seven children and an eighth in prison

Troup, Captain Colin, a prisoner and go-between for Akbar Khan and Pollock

Victoria, Queen, reigned 1837–1901

Wade, Captain then Major Hamlet, brigade-major at Jalalabad

Wade, Mrs, a scandalous sergeant's wife who betrayed the captive soldiers

Waller, Lieutenant Robert Waller, artillery and wife, prisoners when she had a baby

Walsh, Captain Thomas, hostage in Kabul

Wellington, Arthur Wellesley, Duke of

Whiting, Reverend, chaplain to Governor General of India

Wild, Brigadier Charles, joined Nott at Kandahar

Wilson, Bishop Daniel of Calcutta, Metropolitan of India

Woodburn, Captain James, killed at Sidabad, 3 November 1841

Woodhouse, Major Joseph, part of England's force

Wymer, Brigadier George, with Nott at Kandahar, commanded one of his brigades on march to Kabul

Zeman Khan, an elderly relative of Dost Mohammed, briefly proclaimed King of Kabul

Select Bibliography

Primary Sources

Allen, I.N., *Diary of a March Through Sinde and Affghanistan*, London, 1843

Allen, I.N., *Reflections on Portions of the Sermon on the Mount*, 2 parts, London, 1848

Allen, I.N., *Diary of a March Through Sinde and Afghanistan*, n.p., 2002

Carey, Robert, 'Typescript of a letter to his father, Kabul, 7 October, 1842', National Army Museum, 5912-146

Elphinstone, Mountstuart, *An Account of the Kingdom of Caubul and its Dependencies*, 2 vols, London, 1819

Eyre, Lieutenant, V., *Cabul Prisoners*, sketches, London, 1843

Eyre, Lieutenant V., *The Military Operations at Cabul which ended in the Retreat and Destruction of the British Army, January 1842 with a Journal of Imprisonment in Affghanistan*, London, 1843

Gleig, G.R., *Sale's Brigade in Afghanistan: with an account of the seizure and defence of Jalalabad*, London, 1846

Greenwood, J., *The Campaign in Afghanistan*, first published 1844; Stroud, 2005

Illustrated London News, 1842

Lawrence, Lieutenant General Sir George, *Reminiscences of Forty-Three Years in India*, ed. W. Edwards, London, 1875

Low, C.R., *The Afghan War, 1838–42: from the Journal and Correspondence of the late Major-General Augustus Abbott CB Royal (Bengal) Artillery*, London, 1879

Mackenzie, H., *Storms and Sunshine of a Soldier's Life, 1825–1881, Lt. General Colin Mackenzie, CB*, 2 vols, Edinburgh, 1884

Nott's Brigade in Afghanistan, 1838–42, being the private diary of an officer who served in it from first to last, Bombay, 1880

Rawlinson, G., *A Memoir of Major-General Sir Henry Creswicke Rawlinson*, London, New York, Bombay, 1898

Recollections of the First Campaign West of Indus . . . under Major General Sir W. Nott GCB by a Bengal Officer, London, 1845

Sale, Lady, *A Journal of the Disasters in Afghanistan, 1841–2*, London, 1843

Sale, Lady, *Military Memoirs: the First Afghan War*, ed. P. Macrory, London and Harlow, 1969

Stocqueler, J.H., *Memoirs and Correspondence of Major-General Sir William Nott*, 2 vols, London, 1854

Secondary Sources

Bateman, J., *The Life of the Right Reverend Daniel Wilson DD, Late Lord Bishop of Calcutta, Metropolitan of India*, 2 vols, London, 1860

David, S., *The Indian Mutiny 1857*, London, 2003

Edwardes, M., *Playing the Great Game: a Victorian Cold War*, London, 1975

Gibbs, M.E., *The Anglican Church in India*, New Delhi, 1972

Heathcote, T.A., *The Afghan Wars: 1839–1919*, London, 1980

Hensher, P., *The Mulberry Empire*, London, 2003

Hopkirk, P., *The Great Game: On Secret Service in High Asia*, Oxford, 1990

Kaye, J.W., *The History of the War in Afghanistan*, 3 vols, London, 1874

McNally, S.J., 'Chaplains of the East India Company', typescript, 1971

Macrory, P., *Kabul Catastrophe: the invasion and retreat, 1839–1842*, London, 2002

Norris, J.A., *The First Afghan War, 1838–42*, Cambridge, 1967

Palmer, B., *Imperial Vineyard: The Anglican Church in India under the Raj from the Mutiny to Partition*, Sussex, 1999

Sale-Hill, R., 'Major General Sir Robert Sale GCB', *Illustrated Naval and Military Magazine*, vol. 4, 1890, 8–23

Tanner, S., *Afghanistan. A military history from Alexander the Great to the war against the Taliban*, Cambridge, MA, 2009

Venning, A., *Following the Drum: the lives of army wives and daughters*, London, 2006

Whitteridge, G., *Charles Masson of Afghanistan*, Warminster, 1986
Yapp, M.E., *Strategies of British India: Britain, Iran and Afghanistan, 1798–1850*, Oxford, 1980

Index